# A. Philip Randolph

# The African American History Series

**Series Editors:**
Jacqueline M. Moore, Austin College
Nina Mjagkij, Ball State University

Traditionally, history books tend to fall into two categories: books academics write for each other, and books written for popular audiences. Historians often claim that many of the popular authors do not have the proper training to interpret and evaluate the historical evidence. Yet, popular audiences complain that most historical monographs are inaccessible because they are too narrow in scope or lack an engaging style. This series, which will take both chronological and thematic approaches to topics and individuals crucial to an understanding of the African American experience, is an attempt to address that problem. The books in this series, written in lively prose by established scholars, are aimed primarily at nonspecialists. They focus on topics in African American history that have broad significance and place them in their historical context. While presenting sophisticated interpretations based on primary sources and the latest scholarship, the authors tell their stories in a succinct manner, avoiding jargon and obscure language. They include selected documents that allow readers to judge the evidence for themselves and to evaluate the authors' conclusions. Bridging the gap between popular and academic history, these books bring the African American story to life.

**Volumes Published**
*Booker T. Washington, W.E.B. Du Bois, and the Struggle for Racial Uplift*
Jacqueline M. Moore
*Slavery in Colonial America, 1619-1776*
Betty Wood
*African Americans in the Jazz Age: A Decade of Struggle and Promise*
Mark Robert Schneider
*A. Philip Randolph: A Life in the Vanguard*
Andrew E. Kersten

# A. Philip Randolph

*A Life in the Vanguard*

Andrew E. Kersten

**ROWMAN & LITTLEFIELD PUBLISHERS, INC.**
Lanham • Boulder • New York • Toronto • Plymouth, UK

ROWMAN & LITTLEFIELD PUBLISHERS, INC.

Published in the United States of America
by Rowman & Littlefield Publishers, Inc.
A wholly owned subsidiary of The Rowman & Littlefield Publishing Group, Inc.
4501 Forbes Boulevard, Suite 200, Lanham, Maryland 20706
www.rowmanlittlefield.com

Estover Road, Plymouth PL6 7PY, United Kingdom

Copyright © 2007 by Rowman & Littlefield Publishers, Inc.

*All rights reserved.* No part of this publication may be reproduced, stored in a retrieval system, or transmitted in any form or by any means, electronic, mechanical, photocopying, recording, or otherwise, without the prior permission of the publisher.

British Library Cataloguing in Publication Information Available

**Library of Congress Cataloging-in-Publication Data**

Kersten, Andrew Edmund, 1969–
  A. Philip Randolph : a life in the vanguard / Andrew E. Kersten.
  p. cm. — (The African American history series)
  ISBN-13: 978-0-7425-4897-8 (cloth : alk. paper)
  ISBN-10: 0-7425-4897-X (cloth : alk. paper)
  ISBN-13: 978-0-7425-4898-5 (pbk. : alk. paper)
  ISBN-10: 0-7425-4898-8 (pbk. : alk. paper)
  1. Randolph, A. Philip (Asa Philip), 1889– 2. African Americans—Biography. 3. Civil rights workers—United States—Biography. 4. Labor unions—United States—Officials and employees—Biography. 5. Brotherhood of Sleeping Car Porters—History. 6. African Americans—Civil rights—History—20th century. 7. Civil rights movements—United States—History—20th century. I. Title.

E185.97.R27K47 2007
323.092—dc22                                                              2006024150

Printed in the United States of America

∞™ The paper used in this publication meets the minimum requirements of American National Standard for Information Sciences—Permanence of Paper for Printed Library Materials, ANSI/NISO Z39.48-1992.

# Contents

|  |  |  |
|---|---|---|
| | Preface | vii |
| | Acknowledgments | ix |
| | Chronology | xi |
| Chapter 1 | From Preacher Son to Socialist Radical: Randolph's Formative Years in Florida and New York City | 1 |
| Chapter 2 | A Union Revolution: The Creation of the Brotherhood of Sleeping Car Porters | 25 |
| Chapter 3 | When Negroes Don't March: A. Philip Randolph and the Power of Protest Politics during World War II | 47 |
| Chapter 4 | Unfinished Business: Randolph's Civil Rights Struggles during the Cold War | 69 |
| Chapter 5 | The 1963 March on Washington: Randolph's Finest Hour | 91 |
| | Afterword | 115 |
| | Note on Sources | 119 |

Bibliography of Primary Sources        123
Index                                  161
About the Author                       169

# Preface

> So I got this from my father, that you must not be concerned about yourself alone in this world. . . . You must be concerned about things that are far more constructive and far more valuable to mankind and to all peoples than just making money.
>
> —A. Philip Randolph, 1972[1]

Asa Philip Randolph died in 1979, only four years after American troops had evacuated Vietnam, and five years after President Richard M. Nixon resigned from office. Randolph's life ended in an age that to many Americans now seems alien. As historians say, the past has a way of becoming a foreign country. And thus except in academic and some other circles, Americans generally have forgotten Randolph. There is no A. Philip Randolph Day as there is for other civil rights leaders or famous politicians. But Randolph's life is worth remembering, pondering, and interpreting. He was a political radical, a civil rights activist, a labor leader, and an advocate for progressive change in the United States. He spent his adult life grappling with the core problems that dominated twentieth-century America: racism and the struggles of American workers to improve their economic conditions. What connects us to Randolph is his struggle to eliminate bigotry and reform the plight of those who toil near or at the bottom of the economic ladder. In short, Randolph's struggles remain our struggles. Because of the magnitude of Randolph's work—his accomplishments and even his failures—students of history must examine and analyze the historical meanings of his career as a radical and social reformer. Hence, this is a critical and analytical biography. It is an instructive tale about a man and his mission to make the United States live up to its democratic ideals. Randolph never believed he was alone in this quest. Rather, he always saw himself leading a vanguard of reformers destined to rid America of prejudice, discrimination, and poverty. Although he never fully attained those goals, he nonetheless greatly advanced the causes of justice, equality, and equity. For that, he deserves a place of preeminence in American history.

## Note

1. "Reminiscences of A. Philip Randolph," 11 July 1972, Columbia University Oral History Research Office Collection, 79.

# Acknowledgments

First and foremost, I would like to thank Nina Mjagkij and Jackie Moore, the series editors and my good friends, for asking me to write this book. They offered constant encouragement and improved the manuscript tremendously with their comments and criticisms. They also saved me from several historical, grammatical, and typographical errors. Laura Roberts Gottlieb, my editor at Rowman & Littlefield Publishers, was also very helpful, as was her colleague Andrew Boney, an assistant editor at the press. Additionally, I want to thank Professor Roger Daniels for his support and for sharing with me his stories about A. Philip Randolph and Bayard Rustin. He also read the entire manuscript and improved my prose and thoughts greatly. Finally, I need to thank Vickie Kersten and Fred Kersten for reading parts of the manuscript, as well as my University of Wisconsin, Green Bay, colleagues for their support, especially Andrew Austin, Harvey Kaye, Craig Lockard, and Kim Nielsen. And I owe a special debt of thanks to my dear friend Jerry Podair of Lawrence University. Look for his biography of Bayard Rustin in this series.

I dedicate this book to my children, Bethany and Emily. I hope that their generation rediscovers Randolph and picks up his quest for a just and equitable society. It is because of you two that I have hope for the future.

# Chronology

| | |
|---|---|
| April 15, 1889 | Asa Philip Randolph is born in Crescent City, Florida. |
| 1907 | Randolph graduates from the Cookman Institute. |
| 1911 | He and his friend Beaman Hearn move to Harlem. Randolph enrolls in the City College of New York, and he joins the Epworth League and helps to form the Independent Political Council. |
| 1914 | While working for the Brotherhood of Labor, Randolph meets Lucille Green, who is six years older than him. They marry in November. |
| 1916 | Chandler Owen and Randolph join the Socialist Party. |
| 1917 | Randolph and Owen begin to publish the *Hotel Messenger*. By the end of the year, they were publishing the magazine simply as the *Messenger*. |
| 1918 | Randolph and Owen are arrested for sedition, and U.S. Attorney General A. Mitchell Palmer labels the *Messenger* "by long odds the most dangerous of all the Negro publications" in the United States. |
| 1925 | Randolph helps establish the Brotherhood of Sleeping Car Porters (BSCP). |

| | |
|---|---|
| 1928 | The *Messenger* ceases publication. The BSCP grows to a membership of 1,400. |
| 1929 | The BSCP joins the American Federation of Labor. |
| 1932 | The BSCP membership falls to under 800. |
| 1935 | Randolph becomes the president of the National Negro Congress. |
| 1937 | The BSCP wins its struggle with the Pullman Company and becomes the bargaining agent for porters. |
| 1940 | Randolph resigns from the National Negro Congress. |
| 1941 | Randolph's call for a march on Washington results in President Franklin D. Roosevelt's issuing Executive Order 8802 and the creation of the Fair Employment Practice Committee (FEPC). This 1941 march does not take place. |
| 1943 | Randolph establishes the National Council for a Permanent FEPC. |
| 1946 | The wartime FEPC ceases to exist. Randolph helps create the National Education Committee for a New Party and arranges for the publication of the group's "Provisional Declaration of Principles." |
| 1947 | Randolph creates the Committee Against Jim Crow in Military Service and Training to desegregate the military. |
| 1948 | President Truman signs the Universal Military Service and Training Act, and Randolph forms the League for Non-Violent Civil Disobedience Against Military Segregation. President Harry S. Truman issues Executive Order 9980, which creates a new fair employment board for the federal government and Executive Order 9981, which mandates military integration. |
| 1957 | Randolph helps to stage the Prayer Pilgrimage for Freedom, the largest civil rights protest in Washington, D.C., to that date. |

| | |
|---|---|
| 1958 | Randolph organizes the Youth March for Integrated Schools, to support the desegregation of educational institutions. |
| 1959 | Randolph assumes the presidency of the Negro American Labor Council to fight for reform and civil rights in the American Federation of Labor. Randolph stages a second Youth March for Integrated Schools. |
| 1963 | Randolph helps to organize the March on Washington for Jobs and Freedom. |
| 1964 | President Lyndon B. Johnson bestows the Medal of Freedom on Randolph. |
| 1965 | Civil rights and labor leaders establish the A. Philip Randolph Institute to carry on Randolph's legacy. Bayard Rustin is the institute's first director. |
| 1966 | Randolph proposes his Freedom Budget to Congress and President Johnson. |
| May 16, 1979 | Randolph dies in New York City at the age of ninety. |

CHAPTER ONE

# From Preacher Son to Socialist Radical: Randolph's Formative Years in Florida and New York City

> But if someone tried to deprive you of your rights, you've got to resist it. You've got to resent it. You've got to fight against it. [1]
>
> —A. Philip Randolph, 1972

Asa Philip Randolph was born on April 15, 1889, in Crescent City, Florida, to Reverend James W. and Elizabeth Randolph. From the moment he entered this world, one fact dominated his life: he was black. Had he been white, Asa most certainly would have led quite a different life. Among Southern whites, Randolph was a prestigious last name that meant money and power. By contrast, the black Randolphs, many of whom had been slaves of the white Randolphs, never had much money, political power, or social prestige. Being African American severely limited Asa's and his family's access to political, social, economic, and educational opportunities. It shaped their lives and hemmed in their aspirations. Asa Philip Randolph's life story is about breaking the chains that bound him and creating opportunities for himself and for others who suffered poverty and racial discrimination.

Asa inherited his zeal for justice from his father. James was born in 1864 during a period of rapid and historic change, one that was particularly promising for African Americans. Amelia Randolph, Asa's grandmother, had given birth to James at the tail end of the Civil War and at the dawn of a "new" South, when many Americans sought to create political democracy and economic opportunities where there had once been only racial oppression. During Reconstruction, Presidents Abraham Lincoln and Ulysses S.

Grant made some progress in forging a democratic New South. Although it is now common for historians to see Reconstruction as an unfinished revolution, there is no denying the widespread, positive impact that Northern politicians, missionaries, and migrants had upon the region.

The gains after the Civil War were not unalloyed, but they were significant. The Freedman's Bureau, the primary agency charged with helping African Americans make the transition from slavery to freedom, met with varying success, due in part to the widespread—sometimes violent—opposition to black civil rights. This was especially true with the bureau's schools. Nonetheless, many former slaves took advantage of the new educational opportunities. Asa Randolph's father was a case in point. Northern Methodist missionaries provided James and thousands of other former slaves with a solid education. James was a quick study, which was something of a family trait, and he was a popular student among his teachers who provided religious instruction along with the fundamentals of reading, writing, and arithmetic. His Northern benefactors also arranged for him to have an apprenticeship as a tailor. By his early twenties, James was a successful clothier. But cutting cloth was not his calling; rather, he had a call to preach.

It is easy to see why James would be attracted to Methodism, the religion of his teachers. Methodism traditionally appealed to those of humble means. Methodist preachers led austere lives and emphasized plain living, self-discipline, and mutual support. They also championed various causes for justice including the antislavery movement. In the United States, Methodists were frontline abolitionists. In the postslavery era, they refocused their attention on the South by helping people escape the poverty, both spiritual and economic, which had gripped their lives.

James became a preacher in the African Methodist Episcopal Church, which had a much more radical spiritual outlook. The AME Church got its start in Philadelphia at the end of the eighteenth century and propelled Methodism along a trajectory of racial equality. Reverend James Randolph's first appointment came in 1884, only a few months after he was ordained. The position was in Baldwin, Florida, a town located about twenty miles west of Jacksonville. Twenty years old, James felt at home and easily made friends. The tall, thin, black man with a deep and powerful voice was refined and charismatic. Only a year after arriving in Baldwin, he fell in love with and married his sweetheart, Elizabeth Robinson.

In May 1887, Elizabeth gave birth to the Randolphs' first son, James William, Jr. Two years later, their second son, Asa, was born. James, Sr., named him after an Old Testament king who was noted for his altruism and selflessness. Asa Philip Randolph certainly lived up to his namesake's qualities.

By the time Asa was born, his parents had moved from Baldwin to Crescent City, about sixty miles south of Jacksonville. Like Baldwin, Crescent City was a New South boomtown. Positioned along the growing railroad lines, the town supplied the region and the nation with lumber and turpentine. Despite abundant economic opportunities, the Randolphs struggled financially. Although popular, James failed to rise in the AME church hierarchy. He did not have the intellectual or genealogical pedigree to become the rector of a large congregation, let alone a bishop. Reverend Randolph was also more radical than most black ministers. In his sermons, James was something of an early black nationalist arguing that both Jesus and Moses were men of color, a message most certainly welcome among his black parishioners. But James Randolph never served in a big church. What this meant to his family was that they had a hard time making ends meet. In 1891, he and Elizabeth uprooted the family and went to Jacksonville to seek a more prosperous future.

Jacksonville, a port city along the St. Johns River, was an epicenter of the New South and fast becoming a major city. But without much money, the Randolphs moved into the toughest part of town, renting a small two-story house on Jesse Street. Though happy, the family was always in debt and short of the necessities of life. James did not care too much about money and never worried about the family finances. Much to Elizabeth's chagrin, James did not even get upset if the church failed to pay him. To make up for monthly shortfalls, James and Elizabeth diligently kept a large backyard garden as well as a few chickens and hogs. They also started a few businesses to raise extra money. Spurred by Elizabeth, the entrepreneur in the relationship, James opened a laundry, which was about as successful as James' meat market and wood-selling businesses. Asa later recalled the market with some fondness. Despite the poverty, he remembered that at least for a time the family ate well.

Education was a focal point for both James, Jr., and Asa. Reverend Randolph always made sure that the boys had plenty to read, and the family library was small but excellent. Growing up, the Randolph boys were exposed to Charles Dickens, John Keats, Jane Austen, Charles Darwin, and William Shakespeare. Those early days in the parlor and on the front porch had an enormous influence on Randolph. A neighborhood friend, Beaman Hearn, recalled years later that "those boys did practically nothing but read. Matter of fact, if Asa and I were burying a cat behind the house, he wanted to read a service."[2] Both Randolph boys impressed their teachers. Although James, gifted in languages and in mathematics, was the better student, Asa was no slouch. Eventually Reverend James and Elizabeth sent their boys to the

Cookman Institute. James was sixteen and Asa was fourteen, and both flourished at the school. Cookman was a carryover from Reconstruction days. Established by Northern Methodists for the freedmen's children, it had an equal mix of white missionary and local black teachers. The school emphasized a classical education, including instruction in Greek, Latin, French, philosophy, literature, music, forensics, and the natural sciences. It also taught its students the basic trades such as shoemaking, tailoring, husbandry, printing, and home economics.

Asa, who developed his father's baritone voice and exacting diction, excelled at public speaking, singing, and drama. But that was not all. At Cookman, Asa came into his own and out of the shadow of his brilliant brother. By the time he graduated—as class valedictorian, no less—he had mastered all subjects, developed a significant stage presence, become a star baseball player, and was popular with female students.

James, Sr., and Elizabeth also made sure that they gave their boys a solid moral education. Religion was vitally important to both Asa's father and mother. Asa described Grandma Robinson, Elizabeth's mother, as "super-religious." His mother followed in her mother's footsteps. Church and Sunday school attendance were of course mandatory. Moreover, any moral infraction, such as playing cards or marbles, was met with swift corporal punishment. Randolph described his maternal grandmother as "a sort of tyrannical ruler," and it appears that Elizabeth inherited some of that.[3] Unsurprisingly, the boys looked to their dad for softer moral guidance. James, Sr., taught by example: he was an extraordinarily honest man. In 1892, he began raising funds for a new permanent AME church, first named New Hope AME Chapel and later renamed Greater New Hope Chapel. One of the main fundraisers was the Saturday night fish and chicken fry. After each event, Reverend Randolph provided a full financial accounting for every piece of chicken and fish that had been fried.

The young Randolph's moral education also included a clear understanding of American race relations. Both James, Jr., and Asa grew up at a critical moment when the South was becoming segregated. Although it was true that during slavery blacks and whites had at times led separate lives, there was a lot of contact between them. In the New South, after Reconstruction, whites forged a new society in which blacks and whites lived, learned, and prayed apart. And, it was not just a new custom; it was the law. So-called Jim Crow laws were common in the South and were a central part of the reassertion of white supremacy. Without federal assistance, there was little African Americans could do in the South to resist the new order. Jacksonville was completely segregated.

Nonetheless, James made sure that his sons did not succumb to doubt or self-pity. He told his children that there were many influential men in history who had African roots: the Carthaginian general Hannibal who had led his forces and elephants against the Romans; the working-class American revolutionary Crispus Attucks; the radical abolitionists and rebels Nat Turner, Denmark Vesey, and Toussaint L'Ouverture; and the indomitable, uncompromising, and unrivaled Frederick Douglass. Even lowly Jacksonville, which, as the African American writer James Weldon Johnson once said, was fast becoming "a one hundred percent cracker town," had hired an African American as its sole tax collector.[4] As Randolph recalled:

> I, as a matter of fact, never felt, and my brother never felt, we never felt that we were inferior to any white boy, never had that concept at all, and we were told constantly and continuously that "You are as able, you are as competent, you have as much intellectuality as any individual, any white boy of your age and even older than you are, and you are not supposed to bow and take a back seat for anybody."[5]

But that of course did not stop racism from rearing its ugly head. Two episodes in the family's history illustrate the racial system in Jacksonville and the New South. Asa's first exposure to the Southern racial code came one day when he was tagging along with his dad on a trip to return some clothes that his father had repaired. The client was a local sawmill's white foreman, and James tried to take the clothes to the man's shop. Embarrassed and enraged that a black man would intrude on a white man's place of work, the client chased James and Asa off his property. Crushed, both father and son walked home in silence. A few years later, another event provided Asa with clues as about how the Jim Crow world worked. Late one afternoon, a group of African American men called on James Sr. and whispered something in his ear. James and Elizabeth then exchanged looks. The Reverend got the shotgun from behind the upstairs dresser and gave it to Elizabeth. Then he loaded his pistol and left the house. What had happened was that a black man had been arrested for allegedly raping a white woman and had been thrown in the county jail. Rumors were abounding that a white mob was going to lynch him. Reverend James and his friends went down to the jail to defend the man. After a sleepless and unnaturally long night, Asa was happy beyond belief to see his father walking up the path to the house with a satisfied look of a man who had just saved another person's life. Although there was little chance that the jailed man would have a fair trial, he still was lucky in one respect: he had not been lynched, as was the fate of thousands of African Americans.

In 1907, at eighteen and with his education complete, Asa looked for work. A rigorous college education, advanced degrees, and professional jobs were not the usual options for African Americans. So the Randolph boys found work where they could. The U.S. Post Office in Jacksonville hired James to make special deliveries. Later he became a railroad sleeping car porter for the Pullman Company. Asa landed a job at the Union Life Insurance Company. That his position was highly respected in the black community made little difference to him. Collecting premiums was boring, and he soon left the company. There was nothing else waiting, and Asa floated from job to job. Over the next several months, he worked as a clerk in a grocery store, a delivery-truck driver, a lumberyard log stacker, a wheelbarrow pusher at a fertilizer factory, and finally a water boy for a firm laying railroad track. During these trying months, Asa was sustained by his interests in literature and history, as well as his public speaking. He frequently gave public readings from the Bible, Shakespeare, and the poetry of black poet Paul Lawrence Dunbar. Additionally, what must have kept him going was his belief that his future lay somewhere outside of Jacksonville, outside of a social, economic, and political system that had turned him into a second-class citizen. As a young man, Randolph dreamed about abolishing racial discrimination in America.

Asa's father, however, had different hopes for his younger son. To many men of the cloth, the idea of a son succeeding them in the pulpit is attractive. The Reverend James had given up on James, Jr., who despite all his intellectual talents was not interested in the least. Moreover, James had rejected his father's faith. But, there was another hope: Asa. His father believed that his second son would be an ideal minister because of his popularity and speaking ability. James, Sr., wanted Asa not merely to stir people spiritually but to help black Jacksonvillians who were living under oppression. Although Asa shared his father's passion for racial equality, he also questioned the relevance, importance, and reality of religion. He could never be a minister.

Asa and James must have known that they were disappointing their parents and felt that they still owed them something. One day, Reverend James came home and announced that it was time that the boys got religion. This meant that James and Asa would have to go to church and visibly demonstrate that they had turned their lives over to Christ. That the boys seemed a little offtrack spiritually did not reflect well on their father and even less so on their mother, who felt embarrassed in front of the congregation and in front of her mother, the spiritual center of the extended family. So, Asa and James devised a clever plan. One Sunday evening, at the end of his sermon, Reverend Randolph called for witnesses who could testify to Jesus's work in their lives. The brothers shared a wink, fell out of the pews with their fellow parishioners, and cried, yelled, and flailed on the ground. In grand fashion, they ended up at the prayer rail to testify further. Elizabeth hugged them all the way home. The chances are good that Asa's parents knew exactly what had occurred, but they were satisfied.

Clearly the spiritual world held no interest for Asa. Rather, he was caught up in the very earthly concerns about the future of African Americans in the United States. At the turn of the twentieth century, two men dominated the public debate: the conservative Booker T. Washington and the outspoken William Edward Burghardt (W. E. B.) Du Bois. Asa was not attracted to Washington's conservative views. It was the writings of Washington's public nemesis, Du Bois, that caused Randolph to change his life plans, move to Harlem, New York, and become a radical activist.

Not unsurprisingly, the bookish Randolph became a Du Bois adherent after reading *The Souls of Black Folk* (1903), a work that incited social and political movements and caused its author to become a cultural icon. In his book, Du Bois boldly predicted that the essential "problem of the twentieth century is the problem of the color-line."[6] In brilliant essays, he wrote about the importance of the African American past and the vibrancy of black culture and religion. Moreover, he offered a devastating critique of American racism and those who called upon African Americans to accept the inequities in America but nonetheless strive toward economic well-being. Du Bois' most poignant and pointed criticism was directed at Booker T. Washington, the most recognizable African American leader at the turn of the twentieth century.

—Washington's public position was that blacks should not oppose segregation or discrimination but should accept racial conditions and work quietly at acquiring vocational skills to gain the respect of whites. Although Washington secretly worked to tear down the Jim Crow laws that had spread through the New South like wildfire, his philosophy split the African American community in the United States. The Reverend James Randolph was a product of the Washingtonian education process, and at various times James's skills as a tailor had helped put food on the family's table. And yet, James followed Du Bois. Deep down he resented the segregated world that emerged after Reconstruction. He hated the rise of racist politics and disenfranchisement in the South and across the United States. While James never publicly challenged Washington, he also did not stop his sons from reading *The Souls of Black Folk*. The book had an enormous influence upon the twenty-two-year-old Asa. Asa could see the practicality in Washington's view, but he became devoted to Du Bois' ideas, which blazed a path for uplift and achievement and which refused to settle for anything short of equality. Du Bois openly criticized Washington and thereby challenged Washington's previously undisputed position as the spokesperson for African Americans in the United States. In *The Souls of Black Folk*, he argued that Washington had in effect emasculated black men and that he cared more about the money than the higher aims of life. Du Bois concluded that Washington's work, and particularly his 1895 Atlanta speech, only made Washington the most distinguished Southerner since Jefferson Davis, the ex-president of the defunct Confederacy.

To Asa, these words were mind opening. To chase Du Bois' dream Asa knew—as his parents must have known—that he had to get out of Jacksonville and out of the South. There was no question where a budding black radical had to go. The next chance Asa saw he left for Harlem. In the spring of 1911, the twenty-two-year-old Asa and his neighborhood buddy Beaman Hearn boarded a steamer bound for New York City. James, Sr., must have looked upon Asa's departure with mixed feelings. He wanted his second son to follow in his footsteps, become an AME preacher, and perhaps succeed him in the pulpit. But James surely remembered that when he was twenty years old he too had ventured off to find himself. Thus, with some sadness and maybe with a little envy, he helped Asa and Beaman, who had no money, to pay for tickets for their trip north on a steamboat. Reverend Randolph had arranged for the boys to work in the galley—the so-called glory hole—washing dishes in exchange for their passage. They arrived in April 1911 in a New York City that was awash in a flood of political and cultural currents that were reshaping the city's and even America's social landscape.

After the Civil War, New York City continued to be a primary destination for European immigrants and many American migrants. In 1907, almost one and a half million Europeans came to the United States; most of them were first welcomed by the Statue of Liberty and then processed at Ellis Island before landing on Manhattan Island. African Americans also traveled to New York City and other northern destinations by the tens of thousands. Most participants in this Great Migration, as historians have labeled it, had come from former Confederate states and were fleeing the reestablishment of white supremacy. Life under Jim Crow was unbearable for some who sought what they thought were greener pastures in the states that had supplied the soldiers for the Union Army. Others left the New South because of the reign of terror that murderous, vigilante organizations like the Knights of the Ku Klux Klan instigated. Booker T. Washington observed that for every lynching a score of black southerners left for the North. Many of those black migrants headed for New York City. At the time of Randolph's arrival, over 60,000 blacks were living in the city, many of them in Harlem. This is where the

*A. Philip Randolph, ca. 1911, Library of Congress, Prints & Photographs Division, A. Philip Randolph Papers, LCPP003B-43631.*

young Randolph settled and began to transform American labor and race relations.

In Harlem, Randolph was also close to Du Bois, his idol. Randolph also knew that something special was happening there. He had kept track of fellow black Jacksonvillians—and soon-to-be intellectual and cultural luminaries—the brothers J. Rosamond and James Weldon Johnson, who had preceded Randolph by a few years. The Johnson men had made names for themselves in quick order. James Weldon Johnson was a brilliant and influential writer and literary critic, and J. Rosamond was a renowned musician and actor. Both were living proof that the world outside Jacksonville, and outside the New South, offered the freedom to express oneself. Randolph found this possibility appealing.

Asa and Beaman rented an apartment on Harlem's 132nd Street for $1.50 a week. Immediately they began to enjoy the pleasures of urban life. There was of course the hallowed New York City Public Library. Randolph was in heaven there and often read while walking—sometimes out loud—down Lenox Avenue. Then there was the Hippodrome on 45th Street where for a quarter he could spend an entire day watching vaudeville shows. Randolph was also smitten with the stage plays. Nearly every aspect of city life appealed to Randolph, save perhaps the jazz, which he never cared for. But he was perceptive enough to understand that the large number of jazz clubs signaled the presence of a movement of enormous historical significance.

Like all of New York City, and in fact many parts of the United States, Harlem had become a hotbed of political radicalism. It was socialism that ignited the political imaginations of many people, including A. Philip Randolph. Socialism, a worldview that writers, thinkers, and activists like Karl Marx developed, was a response to the political and economic transformations of the nineteenth century, especially industrialization, which in addition to new industries and consumer goods had created devastating poverty, human exploitation, and depravity in the cities of Europe. The rich and powerful in Europe had changed society and created an industrial working class. It was this group, Marx believed, that held the keys to the future. Or as he put it bluntly, the capitalists had given rise to their own grave diggers. The impoverished masses, Marx predicted, would someday form a group, rise up, and transform the world. These winners of the class struggle would then fashion a new reality based upon a dictatorship of the working class, called the proletariat. Once established, this socialist government would then meet the people's needs and compensate everyone's labor justly. Moreover, a socialist government would make sure that the nation, its places of work, and its people were safe, secure, healthy, and educated.

Marx's ideas found fertile ground in the United States. In the nineteenth century, progressive intellectuals as well as radical unionists found socialism very attractive. Labor leaders such as Samuel Gompers and Eugene V. Debs were transformed after reading Marxist ideas. But the energy that socialism unleashed in the United States did not foster a single political and social movement. Rather, in America, socialists split into various groups and factions, some willing to work together, some not. Some were radical while others were willing to accommodate and work within the established capitalist order. Generally speaking, there were three broad categories: the Lassalleans (adherents of Ferdinand Lassalle), who sought to use the existing political and governmental structures to bring about socialist reforms; Marxists were more radical and called for the creation of a political party, which would take power and reshape the United States through democratic means. The last and most radical group were the syndicalists and later the Bolsheviks, or communists, who sought to take power through any means necessary. Randolph eschewed the last two groups and became something of a Lassallean.

In the early 1910s, New York City—specifically Greenwich Village—was home to a socialist intelligentsia in the United States as well as the headquarters of various socialist organizations. It was the golden age of American socialism when activists, organizers, thinkers, writers, and politicians worked side by side, if not together, in an attempt to change the economic, political, and social order.

It was this New York City, on the cutting edge of political, social, and cultural revolutions, that Randolph entered. He and Hearn spent their first few weeks taking in New York City's sights and sounds. However, rather quickly they ran out of money. Fortunately, the city offered plenty of employment opportunities for African Americans. Job discrimination did exist, but it was not as oppressive as in the South. Paging through the want ads in the *New York World*, they came across a call for porters in an apartment building. Thinking that they were the only two who wanted such a lowly job, they were shocked to find a long line outside the apartment's business office. Faced with the choice of getting the job or going back home, Randolph walked up to the queue and in his baritone voice asked if the men knew how to use a typewriter. In near unison, they said no. "Well, you're wasting your time," Randolph told them. "These people are looking for men who know something about typewriting."[7] After a short time, only Randolph and Hearn were left standing outside the office door. Asa got the lobby switchboard job and Beaman worked the elevator.

Two months later, in October 1911, Beaman announced that he was going back to Jacksonville to honor his promise to his father to return and start a business. For the first time, Asa was completely alone. It is perhaps surprising that he turned to the church for solace. He attended several AME, Methodist, and Baptist churches before finding Salem Methodist on West 133rd Street, which was led by the Reverend Frederick Cullen, father of the great poet Countee Cullen. No religious longing drove Asa to Sunday service. Rather, Salem Methodist was home to the Epworth League, a group of young blacks who shared interests in many things, including theater. Randolph hated the Bible study but loved the acting troupe. His successes onstage in leading roles in *Othello*, *Hamlet*, and *The Merchant of Venice* encouraged him even more to seek his new dream of becoming a famous stage actor. The nationally renowned Harlem actor Henri Strange even encouraged Asa to pursue the theater. Exuberantly, Asa wrote home to tell his mother and father about his new career. His parents' response was chilling: they bluntly told him to stop engaging in immoral behavior. In James and Elizabeth's view, acting rated somewhere near prostitution, drinking, and gambling. Crushed, Asa obediently left the theater.

The sting of his parents' rebuke did not last long. Randolph was never one to wallow in self-pity or self-doubt. Within a few months, he had formed a new organization to fill the void left by his departure from the Epworth League. The Independent Political Council was a collection of politically minded Harlemites who loved to debate current events. Randolph also became a student at the City College of New York (CUNY), enrolling in courses in history, politics, economics, and philosophy. At the time, CUNY did not charge tuition. As Randolph remarked later, it was the only kind of college he could afford. One of the most important professors he met was the philosopher Morris R. Cohen, who inspired him. To the political left of most of his colleagues, Cohen made his students question an economic system that created both wealth and poverty in America. To investigate these questions, Randolph turned to Marx. As Randolph was deep in the pages of *Capital*, Marx's most detailed explanation of his ideas, an intellectual light bulb turned on in him. As Randolph said later, he read "Marx as children read *Alice in Wonderland*."[8] He began to read more Marxist and socialist writers. Suddenly, his world started to make sense. Racism and discrimination were not merely a part of the American social character. Rather, they were part of a broader system of social control that split the working class into smaller, more easily exploited groups. Thus, the African American struggle was every worker's struggle, and the converse was true as well. Suddenly, Randolph's mission in life became clear. By the spring of 1914, Randolph was devoting himself to the socialist cause. In practical terms, this meant that he was going to do three things: organize unions for exploited workers, enter the rough-and-tumble world of New York politics, and motivate African Americans so that they could strive for economic and political independence. The last goal was extraordinarily important to Randolph's socialist outlook. In the lingo of the day, he wanted to create a vanguard—an advanced group of activists—who would energize the campaign for worker and minority rights and inspire others to join.

Randolph's initial attempts to organize socialist unions failed. While employed briefly aboard the steamship *Paul Revere*, he unsuccessfully tried to establish a union of black waiters. Ever since he had sailed from Jacksonville, he longed to improve the lives of those toiling away in the glory holes of ships, where African American workers lived, gambled, and bathed. His efforts to organize black porters at the Consolidated Gas Company met a similar fate. By the summer of 1914, Asa was a struggling socialist union organizer. He was continually down on his luck, with no claim to fame and, more importantly, no regular means of income. But once again, Randolph was down but not out.

In the late spring of 1914, after a public debate sponsored by the Independent Political Council, one of Randolph's old Epworth League friends, Ernest T. Welcome, approached him with a job offer. Welcome operated a Harlem employment agency that which catered to African American migrants from the South and West Indian immigrants, most of whom were considered "black" in the United States. The employment office, the Brotherhood of Labor, had two equally vital missions. First, it found work for Harlem's newest arrivals. Second, Welcome wanted the Brotherhood of Labor to serve as an educating and unifying force in the community. But for that work he needed Randolph's help. Welcome wanted him to design political pamphlets, posters, and handbills to introduce and indoctrinate black newcomers to Harlem's cultural and political life.

Working for Welcome's Brotherhood appealed to Randolph; the job dovetailed nicely with his political outlook. A budding socialist, Asa believed firmly that economic concerns trumped racial ones. Yet he also was firmly convinced that African Americans had to unite to fight for the economic and political betterment of their race and the rest of American society. Asa also loved his job for a more earthly reason. A very attractive thirty-one-year-old widow named Lucille Green worked down the hall from his office. At twenty-five, Randolph did not have much to offer beyond exuberance. But youthfulness was exactly what Lucille was looking for.

Born Lucille Campbell in 1883 in Christianburg, Virginia, she had received a college education at Howard University, where she studied to become a teacher. Popular and good looking, she had several suitors as a young woman. She married another Howard student, Joseph Green, who after graduation found a job as a customs official in New York City. Not long after they arrived, Joseph died. The sudden death of her husband was a shattering personal blow that left her questioning her future. In the end, Lucille decided to leave her teaching position and go back to school. Taking advantage of the brand-new cosmetology school set up by the incredibly successful black entrepreneur, Madame C. J. Walker, Lucille graduated quickly and opened her own salon in Harlem. Lucille's association with Madame Walker not only brought her financial success, but it also brought her into the world of the

*Lucille Randolph, ca 1920, Library of Congress, Prints & Photographs Division, A. Philip Randolph Papers, LC-USZ62-97536.*

black upper middle class. Wealth and status, however, did not bring her complete happiness. When Asa finally got the courage to ask Lucille on a date, they hit it off immediately. They had lots in common, including a birthday, April 15. Yet, they were an odd couple, a strange mix: poor and rich; shy Asa and gregarious Lucille; and at least initially socialist and capitalist. But sometimes opposites attract. Their love for each other was legendary.

In November 1914, Lucille and Asa were married. Randolph had not wanted a church wedding but eventually agreed, and the wedding took place at St. Philips's Episcopal Church. Lucille, or "Buddy" as Asa called her and she called him, supported her socialist husband both spiritually and financially. Randolph did not design his union and political endeavors to make him rich. In fact, they always cost more than they took in. Thanks to Lucille, he could eat and he had a warm bed every night. He now had the money to become America's leading black radical, and create his vanguard for socialist reform.

In 1915, Randolph rededicated himself to his political work. Unlike in his previous attempts to organize African American workers and to fight for a socialist future, he was no longer alone. Although never quite comfortable in large groups, Asa always needed partners to transform his dreams into reality. Lucille, of course, provided much of that support. In addition, Randolph met Chandler Owen in 1915, and for the next ten years they would be collaborators in their socialist quest. Randolph had met Chandler at one of those Harlem socialite parties that he detested. The two became instant friends. Chandler was just ten days older than Randolph. Both were radicals and loved to argue about socialism. Both were very bright and well read. Randolph took credit for introducing Owen to Marx, and Owen claimed that he had introduced Randolph to Lester Frank Ward, the progressive sociologist who had written several influential works arguing against social Darwinism and for active government intervention to solve social problems. Both joined the Socialist Party in 1916, and generally were inseparable. But they did make an odd couple. Whereas Asa was tall, thin, and debonair, Owen was short and rather portly. Moreover, unlike Randolph, Chandler never married and loved parties. He was a drinker and a gambler. They nonetheless made a productive team.

The black socialist duo started drawing Harlem's attention quickly. Frequently, in 1915 and 1916, they appeared on street corners delivering speeches on soapboxes. In particular, people noticed Randolph. In short order, he drew large crowds. When the New York City police thought that the crowds were too large, they used their billy clubs to disperse them. The quick-thinking Randolph devised a successful method to stop the policemen—many of whom were Irish—from harassing him. As soon as he saw them closing in, he began talking about "the oppression of the Irish people by British imperialism."[9] The policemen actually stopped to listen and left the crowd alone. Once in the clear, Randolph resumed his speech on racial discrimination and the benefits of socialism.

It was not long before Asa and Chandler found something better than street-side socialism. In 1917, while looking for a larger office for the Independent Political Council, the two ran into William White, the president of the Headwaiters and Sidewaiters Society of Greater New York. White had

Chandler Owen, ca. 1942, Library of Congress, Prints & Photographs Division, Farm Security Administration—Office of War Information Photograph Collection, LC-USF344-091190-B.

heard the two men several times giving speeches on Harlem street corners and wanted them to help organize and advance his union. Specifically, he wanted them to write and edit a magazine for the union, and he offered them free office space, free furniture, and free typewriters. They now had a vehicle for their message, a magazine, which they called Hotel Messenger. Their magazine was an instant hit and drew the two radicals into a much wider circle of friends and political comrades. Among those who regularly dropped by the magazine's office were black writers Fred R. Moore, T. Thomas Fortune, and Randolph's hometown friend James Weldon Johnson. Additionally, a radical cadre of West Indian immigrants frequently stopped by, including St. Croix native Hubert Harrison. A socialist and Harlem's "black Socrates," Harrison became a mentor to both men. But other black Caribbean radicals also contributed to their development: journalist Cyril V. Briggs, poet Claude McKay, and writer and editor W. A. Domingo. The last became Randolph's very good friend and associate.

Randolph, who had now adopted the more dignified sounding name A. Philip Randolph, and Owen published only eight issues of Hotel Messenger. In August 1917, White fired them both. They had published a damning exposé of headwaiters' abuse of sidewaiters. White, who represented the former more than the latter, was outraged. How could these two young turks who worked only because White had offered them employment attack his union and embarrass him publicly? Randolph and Owen were not apologetic but rather proud of their work. They cleared out their office and launched their magazine next door. They did, however, rename it: the Hotel Messenger became the Messenger.

Its editors called the Messenger "the first voice of radical, revolutionary, economic and political action among Negroes in America." And in the beginning, the magazine lived up to its masthead. It was beautifully and lovingly produced, and it expressed radical thoughts in a clear and readable fashion. Regardless of social station or political persuasion, everyone agreed that the Messenger was essential reading. U.S. Attorney General A. Mitchell Palmer thought that Randolph and Owen's magazine was "by long odds the most dangerous of all the Negro publications" and probably considered its editors to be similarly dangerous as well.[10]

The Messenger had two basic goals. First, Randolph and Owen wanted to clear the decks of all other philosophies, politics, and faiths. As they wrote in their first issue:

> Our aim is to appeal to reason, to lift our pens above the cringing demagogy of the times, and above the cheap peanut politics of the old reactionary Negro

leaders. Patriotism has no appeal to us; justice has. Party has no weight with us; principle has. Loyalty is meaningless; it depends on what one is loyal to. Prayer is not one of our remedies; it depends on what one is praying for. We consider prayer as nothing more than a fervent wish; consequently, the merit and worth of a prayer depend upon what the fervent wish is.[11]

The second goal of the magazine was to rally African Americans to radical politics. Randolph knew that this was no easy task. He predicted that being in the black socialist vanguard meant that he might alienate both blacks and whites.

As Randolph and Owen organized their first issue of the *Messenger* in October 1917, they consciously modeled their magazine on the other leading black periodical of the day: the National Association for the Advancement of Colored People's (NAACP) *Crisis*, which had begun in 1910. Intellectually, however, they wanted to distance themselves from the *Crisis* and the other major black magazine, *Opportunity*, which the National Urban League (NUL) had launched in 1923. The difference between the NUL's and NAACP's magazines could not be plainer than their titles. In its magazine, the Urban League stressed the economic and political opportunities that were available and attainable. The NAACP always stressed the struggles of African Americans to achieve civil rights. The *Messenger* distinguished itself from both publications with its radical message.

In the end, running any magazine comes down to dollars and cents. To compete, Randolph and Owen set their issue price at fifteen cents. With that they could barely make ends meet, and they relied heavily upon donations from Jewish socialists who published the *Daily Forward* and from a $10,000 grant that James Weldon Johnson of the NAACP helped secure from the politically liberal Garland Fund. Although the *Messenger* never achieved its editors' goals of laying the groundwork for a socialist future, it did have an impact upon the Harlem Renaissance and upon African American history.

The first opportunity to draw black Harlem to Randolph's socialist vision came late in the summer of 1917 as Randolph and Chandler were sending the first issue of the *Messenger* to the printers. That November, New York City was embroiled in a contentious four-way mayoral election pitting the progressive incumbent "Boy" Mayor John Purroy Mitchel against the Democratic candidate Judge John Hylan, the Republican William Bennet, and the Socialist Morris Hillquit. Born in Latvia in 1869, Hillquit had established himself as one of America's leading and most popular Marxist thinkers by the late nineteenth century. A dedicated union organizer and a fierce critic of the conservative unionism of the American Federation of Labor, Hillquit attacked the leaders of the labor movement before World War I for not reaching out to all workers and for not being more radical in their demands for equality in American life. He personally challenged the American Federation of Labor's (AFL) president Samuel Gompers in a famous 1914 debate in which he urged workers to adopt socialism and not merely join a union. Hillquit was also a savvy politician and central figure in New York City's radical labor and political movements.

As brothers in the cause, Randolph and Owen immediately threw their full support behind Hillquit. In the *Messenger*'s inaugural issue, they listed twenty-five reasons why Harlem's African Americans should vote for Hillquit. The Socialist Party, Randolph and Owen wrote, was the party of the working class and African Americans were mostly of the working class. They argued that Hillquit would improve the lives of African Americans by lowering rents, tolls, and utility costs. In addition to pro-working class bread-and-butter issues, Hillquit advocated a more efficient and just police department that he promised would use more brains than billy clubs. Despite Randolph's and Owen's best efforts to help Hillquit, he lost to his Democratic opponent. Still, Hillquit polled more votes than any socialist mayoral candidate in New York City's history. Some credited the *Messenger* for swinging an estimated 25 percent of the Harlem vote to the Socialist. Randolph and Owen had made a difference, but it was not enough.

Aside from city politics, Randolph and Owen sought to convince their readers to oppose American entry into World War I. Here they were following the Socialist Party line. In 1917, at an emergency meeting in St. Louis, the Socialist Party had resolved to oppose the European war, which had begun in August 1914. But in April 1917, President Woodrow Wilson had brought the United States into the conflict on the side of Great Britain and France. Randolph and Owen shared this position, but they were not blind followers. Randolph firmly believed that pacifism was a logical extension of socialism. In the November 1917 issue of the *Messenger*, Randolph and Owen editorialized against the war, arguing that only capitalists—and not workers—profited from the death and destruction. They called on the "Common Man" to resist the profiteers and their government allies. Using the *Messenger*, Randolph continuously attacked President Wilson and the war effort. He and Chandler also went on a speaking tour to rally black support for the antiwar position. In August 1918, Randolph and Owen appeared in Cleveland, Ohio, at a pacifist rally sponsored in part by local socialist groups. While Owen and several new socialist friends sold the *Messenger* to the assembled crowd, Randolph spoke forcefully against the war and urged civil disobedience. His words had an unintended consequence. After his speech,

U.S. Department of Justice officials, who had secretly infiltrated the assembly, arrested Randolph and Owen and charged them with violating the recently passed the Sedition Act, a law that gave the federal government unparalleled powers to crush legitimate opposition during World War I.

Randolph faced significant jail time for violating the Sedition Act, and federal officials threatened dissenters with immediate frontline duty if they did not toe the line. At the time, though, it was very unlikely that he would be drafted. He had told the New York City draft board that he was the sole supporter of his wife and children. Truthfully, he was not: Lucille was his main means of support. Moreover, Lucille and Asa never had children. The Wilson administration jailed hundreds for opposing the war. Ironically, what saved Randolph was racism. The Cleveland judge who heard his and Owen's case believed the duo to be patsies and questioned whether these men could have been smart enough to become socialist radicals. After two days in jail and a short trial, at which Randolph and Owen were defended by Seymour Stedman, a famous socialist lawyer from Chicago, both were released and they immediately boarded a train for Chicago to address another mass demonstration and sell more issues of the *Messenger*.

Randolph's unconventional stand on the war strengthened his friendship with Eugene V. Debs. Perhaps the greatest American socialist, Debs had become a radical after years of battling employers. His famous 1894 strike against the Pullman Company had convinced him without a doubt that the world was separated between the haves and have-nots. Debs was a martyr for the poor and oppressed. Although he was never, as Randolph put it, "intellectually too vigorous," Debs was a great spiritual leader and mentor.[12] He had aided Randolph with his activities in Harlem, was instrumental in converting Lucille to the socialist cause, and even encouraged her to run for the New York state legislature on the Socialist Party ticket. It was Debs who had invited Randolph to speak in Cleveland. They had all gone to jail together. But while Randolph got out, Debs remained in federal prison until Christmas 1921.

While Randolph's pacifism introduced him to new friends, it also resulted in a rift with others. It was during the war that he stopped idolizing W. E. B. Du Bois. In the July 1918 issue of the *Crisis*, Du Bois urged black Americans "to forget our special grievances and close our ranks shoulder to shoulder with our own white fellow citizens and the allied nations that are fighting for democracy."[13] Harlem radicals reacted to Du Bois' message with shock. Black socialists such as Hubert Harrison and Randolph were incensed, particularly after they learned that the army was planning to commission Du Bois as a captain. Supporting President Wilson, who was no friend of the African

American civil rights movement, was bad enough, but accepting the military position was in Randolph's view total capitulation. In issue after issue, Randolph and Owen attacked Du Bois and the war effort. If Du Bois was so excited about the Great War, they wrote, why did he not "volunteer to go to France . . . to make the world safe for democracy?" Finally, the *Messenger*'s editors concluded that they would rather fight for democracy at home and "make Georgia safe for the Negro"[14] The uproar over the proposed captaincy caused the army to rescind its offer to Du Bois. Because of Randolph's outspoken criticism of President Wilson and the war, the federal government suspended the *Messenger*'s second-class postal status, making the magazine and thus impossible for Randolph and Owen to send to subscribers. Additionally, the Wilson administration punished Randolph by changing his draft status and immediately sent him notice that he was going to be inducted into the army. Luckily, the war ended before he had to go. If it had not, Randolph would have refused to go and was willing to face the consequences.

World War I served to divide, rather than unify, black Americans. Randolph and Owen most certainly had convinced some to support their pacifist and socialist causes and to abandon their support of Du Bois. But there was no clear winner. Moreover, by 1919, there were growing divisions among black radicals and activists. Black leaders across the United States expected that at the end of the war black Americans would be duly rewarded for their patriotic service with full citizenship. Just the opposite happened. In 1919, in twenty cities—both large like Chicago, Illinois, and small like Elaine, Arkansas—whites attacked African American communities in a violent attempt to maintain a racial order that placed blacks at the bottom of society. In Omaha, Nebraska, one of the cities that experienced a race riot, an angry white mob burned the county courthouse to the ground in order to seize a black man accused of attacking a white woman. The group dragged the man through the city's main thoroughfares, shot him more than a thousand times, and hung his mutilated, unrecognizable body in the middle of Omaha's busiest downtown intersection. Blacks responded to the "Red Summer," as James Weldon Johnson called it, with shock, horror, grief, and anger. Poet Claude McKay provided one of the most famous reactions first published in Max Eastman's *Liberator* magazine and later republished in the *Messenger*. In "If We Must Die," McKay expressed the thoughts of many when he wrote: "Like men we'll face the murderous, cowardly pack, / Pressed to the wall, dying but fighting back!"[15]

Most black Americans shared the outrage, particularly Du Bois, who had urged support for Wilson's war efforts. But there was no consensus on a course of action. Du Bois and the NAACP began to work for federal civil rights legislation that would outlaw lynching and other aspects of racial discrimination. Randolph, however, urged black Americans to adopt a completely different kind of strategy. In the *Messenger*, Harlem's "Lenin and Trotsky," as Randolph and Owen were now known, stopped just short of issuing a call to arms. They also made it clear that only socialism could stop lynching and establish fair systems of education, politics, and policing. They heaped praise upon the Bolsheviks who had taken power in Russia, toppling the czar and establishing the Soviet Union.

Marcus Garvey, who had emigrated from Jamaica in 1916, offered another solution to the problems of black America. Garvey and his organization, the Universal Negro Improvement Association (UNIA), argued that the only way for blacks to improve their lives was to leave the United States and resettle in Africa, where they could build their own nation. Initially, Randolph supported Garvey, even literally giving him his soapbox so that a street crowd that had assembled to listen to Randolph could hear the thoughts of this Harlem newcomer. But as time went on, Randolph became one of Garvey's sharpest critics. Garvey had an enormous disdain for the leaders of black America. At first, Garvey aimed his verbal barbs mostly at Du Bois, something that Randolph probably enjoyed privately. But when Garvey began to widen his criticism and began to draw thousands of blacks to his cause, Randolph dropped his support. Publicly he denounced UNIA's back-to-Africa scheme as unworkable and a sideshow. Perhaps Randolph was also a little jealous. After all, he had been working hard to gather the vanguard of the socialist revolution with only meager results. Garvey had popped up, given speeches, held rallies and parades replete with pomp and circumstance, promising a pie-in-the-sky dream about "Negro Zionism," and hundreds of thousands of blacks bought it.

The rapidly rising conflict between Randolph and Garvey reached a peak in 1922 when the news broke that Garvey had been working with the Ku Klux Klan, which also believed that all descendents of Africa should return across the Atlantic Ocean. A flurry of devastating criticism followed in the pages of the *Messenger* as well as the *Crisis*. Du Bois wrote that Garvey was a dangerous enemy of African Americans. Randolph was more colorful, calling Garvey's cause an "erratic rampage" spurred on by a "groundless braggadocio" who gathered his followers by beating the air and "waving his big, fat hands furiously" while yapping senseless plans.[16]

Something in Randolph's tirade struck a nerve. On September 5, 1922, a courier delivered a plain brown paper package to the *Messenger*'s offices. The box contained a severed human hand from a white man and an ominous note:

> Listen Randolph—We have been watching your writings in all your papers for quite a while but we want you to understand before we act. If you are not in favor with your own race movement you can't be with ours. There is no space in our race for you and your creed. . . . We have sent you a sample of our good work, so watch your step or else.[17]

The letter was signed "K.K.K." Randolph, who never seemed to be scared of anyone or anything, published the letter in the *Messenger*'s next issue, charging that the Ku Klux Klan had come to Garvey's rescue.

In 1923, Garvey self-destructed. Federal investigators had examined his passenger and freight shipping company, the Black Star Line, a parody of the famous British company, the White Star Line, which had launched the HMS *Titanic*. Soon, Garvey appeared before a federal judge on charges of fraud and misuse of the mail system. Found guilty in 1925, he was sentenced to five years in prison, but in 1927 President Calvin Coolidge released and deported him. With Garvey's departure, Randolph had essentially won his first political battle. But it was an incomplete victory. By the mid-1920s, he was no closer to a socialist revolution than he had been in 1917. In fact, he was further from it. The *Messenger* was hemorrhaging money. Worse, two-thirds of its subscribers were white radicals, not African Americans. Then in quick succession, Randolph lost his father and his collaborator. In September 1924, Reverend James Randolph died. Shortly thereafter, Chandler left for Chicago and gave up the socialist cause for a more stable middle-class life. The *Messenger* continued for a while, but slowly Randolph had to make strategic sacrifices. To gain advertisers as well as broaden public appeal, he toned down the socialist rhetoric about revolution and radicalism. By 1925, Asa was back where he had begun in 1917: he was nearly penniless and adrift without a cause. However, that was about to change dramatically in the summer of 1925.

## Notes

1. "Reminiscences of Asa Philip Randolph," 11 July 1972, Columbia University Oral History Research Office, 81. Hereinafter, Randolph oral history.

2. Quoted from Jervis Anderson's interview with Beaman Hearn, in Jervis Anderson, *A. Philip Randolph: A Biographical Portrait* (Berkeley: University of California Press, 1972; 1986), 39.

3. Randolph oral history, 5.

4. James Weldon Johnson, *Along This Way: The Autobiography of James Weldon Johnson* (New York: The Viking Press, 1933), 45.

5. Randolph oral history, 73.

6. W. E. B. Du Bois, *The Souls of Black Folk* (New York: Fawcett World Library, 1961), 23.

7. Quoted from Jervis Anderson's interview with A. Philip Randolph, in Anderson's *A. Philip Randolph*, 56.

8. Quoted from Jervis Anderson's interview with A. Philip Randolph, in Anderson's *A. Philip Randolph*, 62.

9. Randolph oral history, 157.

10. Congress, *Investigation Activities of the Department of Justice: Letter from the Attorney General Transmitting in Response to a Senate Resolution of October 17, 1919, A Report on the Activities of the Bureau of Investigation of the Department of Justice Against Persons Advising Anarchy, Sedition, and the Forcible Overthrow of the Government, 17 November 1919*, Senate Documents, 66th Cong., 1st sess., 1919, vol. 12, S. Doc. 153, 172.

11. *Messenger* 1 (November 1917): 1.

12. Randolph oral history, 113.

13. W. E. B Du Bois, "Close Ranks," *Crisis* (July 1918): 111.

14. *Messenger* 2 (1918): 7; Anderson, 101.

15. Sondra Kathryn Wilson, ed., *The Messenger Reader: Stories, Poetry, and Essays from* The Messenger (New York: The Modern Library, 2000), 36.

16. Wilson, *The Messenger Reader*, 351.

17. *Messenger* (October 1922); Anderson, 131; and FBI Report, 23 September 1922, A. Philip Randolph FBI File, no. 100-55616, pt. 1, 1.

CHAPTER TWO

# A Union Revolution: The Creation of the Brotherhood of Sleeping Car Porters

> I've spent my life . . . studying the economic and social history of our group from the days of slavery onward, and I've come to the conclusion that it is not enough to build churches. . . . You have to take that responsibility upon your own shoulders, building something on which you can depend, and not depend on the Pullman Company.
>
> —A. Philip Randolph, 1925[1]

One day in June 1925, A. Philip Randolph silently wandered up Seventh Avenue in Harlem. The *Messenger* was in deep financial trouble. Moreover, Lucille's salon business was suffering, and it was mostly his fault. His radicalism and his antiwar activities had scared patrons away. Of course, Lucille herself had become a socialist, but it was her husband who had angered and offended her clientele. As Randolph crossed 135th Street, a snappily dressed man in a white Panama hat stopped him. Ashley L. Totten was a strong-willed African American railroad worker on his day off. A native of St. Croix in the Virgin Islands, Totten had lived in New York City for ten years. He of course knew of Harlem's great street radical, A. Philip Randolph, and sought him out for help. Totten was a sleeping-car porter for the Pullman Company. After years of enduring discrimination, intimidation, and awful working conditions, Totten and his colleagues decided to form a union for Pullman porters. Having read the *Messenger* for years, he figured that Randolph could help the porters organize.

Totten invited Randolph to speak to a group of porters and tell them about trade unions and collective bargaining. Without hesitating, Randolph agreed, and a few days later he gave quite a stirring speech. Little did Randolph know that his presentation was really a job interview, and he had passed with flying colors. Less than a week later Totten asked Randolph to attend another, this time secret, meeting of Pullman porters. Totten and three co-workers asked Randolph to organize the sleeping car porters. Although hesitant at first, Randolph eventually agreed. His decision not only transformed his life but also the lives of all Pullman porters and those of many Americans. The Brotherhood of Sleeping Car Porters (BSCP) became Randolph's vanguard for reform and together they changed the course of U.S. history.

The story of the Pullman porters began in 1853 with an uncomfortable train trip. George M. Pullman, a twenty-one-year-old building mover and woodworker from Albion, New York, was traveling from Chicago to New York. The last leg of Pullman's trip was at night. Although he had purchased a berth on a sleeper, the experience was singularly uncomfortable. There was no rest for this weary traveler. Lying in his clothes and shoes because the train car was not properly heated, Pullman spent the night thinking of ways to improve the sleeping car. Five years of trial and error resulted in the introduction of the first Pullman sleeping car in 1858. Initially, the major passenger railroads and their customers did not take to these cars. Undeterred, Pullman kept redesigning and building until finally in 1865 he had produced his masterpiece, the "Pioneer." It was not a mere sleeping car; it was a palace car. With carpeted floors, upholstered seats with brocaded fabrics, elegant wood frames, comfortable seats and beds, and the latest heating and lighting systems, the passenger car was a remarkable accomplishment. And yet, like any invention, building it was only half the problem. Pullman needed to market his car, and a unique opportunity came when President Abraham Lincoln was assassinated on April 14, 1865. Pullman provided Lincoln's corpse with the ride back to Illinois and the final resting place. Pullman's "Pioneer" palace sleeping car instantly became famous.

As the orders rushed in, Pullman had to expand his base of operations. By 1880, he had built a new plant outside of Chicago and established an entire town to house his workforce. Pullman, Illinois, was the first planned industrial town of its kind. The workers who lived inside Pullman's 4,000-acre community inhabited a world dominated by their employer. In addition to working for Pullman, they rented Pullman housing, shopped at the Pullman Company store, and paid for everything in official Pullman Company money. Long before Henry J. Ford, George Pullman exemplified the paternalistic

American employer. Workers' lives began and ended according to Pullman's dictates. Although critics and pundits initially lavished praise upon Pullman's model town, which had wide streets, attractive homes, regular city services, and a library, slowly many began to question whether Pullman's benevolence was all that charitable or altruistic. Indeed, Pullman made profits not only from his workers' labors but also from the rents they paid to live in his houses and from their purchases in his stores. Had Pullman always kept his workers' interests and their families at heart, there might not have been much labor unrest in the town. But Pullman was always concerned with profit more than people.

In 1894, in search for profits during a terrible economic depression, Pullman, whose name had become synonymous with luxury, efficiency, and modern living, fired one-third of his work force and reduced by 30 percent the wages of the remaining employees. Moreover, Pullman refused to lower rents in his company town or prices at the company store. Quickly a group of workers, who belonged to the fledgling American Railway Union (ARU), led by the resilient Eugene V. Debs, formed a grievance committee and appealed directly to Pullman. He refused to negotiate and immediately locked out his workers. Meanwhile the ARU voted to strike. While this dispute raged, Pullman brought in a new and nonunion workforce. Fights between the scabs and the union workers prompted a request by U.S. Attorney General Richard Olney, who asked President Grover Cleveland to use federal troops to end the labor conflict. On July 2, 1894, the soldiers arrived. Within a month, Pullman hired strikebreakers, crushed the strike, and defeated the union. Twenty-five unionists died and more than 406 were injured. George Pullman's reputation suffered as a result of the strike, and he was never quite able to recover his position as one of America's greatest and most magnanimous industrial statesmen. There was one group of Americans, however, whose respect for Pullman went nearly unabated: African Americans.

George Pullman had a unique relationship with African Americans. Following the Civil War, he hired thousands of ex-slaves to work as attendants in his palace cars. African Americans accounted for most of Pullman's train employees, although he hired Filipinos and Chinese as well (often to hamper the formation of unions). Symbolically the connections with black workers were quite advantageous. Pullman had helped bury Lincoln, and then he had taken on the challenges of moving African Americans from slavery to freedom. Pullman—and his successor Robert Todd Lincoln, the president's son—hired ex-slaves precisely because black faces still projected the image of servility to white customers. And the jobs that Pullman assigned to his black workforce were those that white conductors did not want: making and taking down beds, carrying luggage, cleaning bathrooms and spittoons, shining shoes, and seeing to every passenger's need. The Pullman Company also employed African American women as maids to tend to the needs of white women traveling alone or with small children. The porters and maids were to do their work quickly, quietly, efficiently, and with a smile and a "yes, sir" and "yes, madam." Loyalty to their employer meant the chance to rise economically. In black communities across the United States, Pullman porters were decidedly middle class, and their uniforms were a badge of accomplishment. African American men wanted to become porters, or as they put it, trade their coveralls for suits. As one porter recalled: "Denims were field cloths, work clothes that reminded the men of slavery; the clean, crisp uniforms of the Pullman porters were seen as genuine status symbols, a major advance."[2] Porters earned a decent wage; they were always sharply dressed; they traveled constantly; and they seemed to possess an urbane sophistication that others only dreamed about. They owed that to the Pullman Palace Car Company.

Indeed, there is no denying that the porter jobs helped some African Americans rise from poverty. By 1915, the Pullman Company was the single largest employer of African Americans. Many famous black Americans began their working lives as porters: the politician Perry Howard, novelist Claude McKay, Morehouse College president Benjamin E. Mays, and famous union organizer Frank Crosswaith. But being a Pullman porter came with an indisputable downside. Being one of "George's boys" meant that porters had to project, at least publicly, that they were docile servants. In fact, this image of the Pullman porter literally sold the sleeping car service. In company advertising, time and time again, Pullman's marketing gurus stressed the porters' efficient, subservient, and unflappable nature. It all started with the name of every black porter. To a man, they were known publicly as "George." Porters hated this practice. Some whites resented it too. In 1916, Chicago lumber merchant George W. Delany formed an all-white protection association, the Society for the Prevention of Calling Sleeping Car Porters George. Eventually the Society claimed 33,000 members, including Georgia's senator Walter F. George, King George V of England, George Cardinal Mundelein, and most significantly George Herman "Babe" Ruth, Jr. As the naming ritual suggests, the Pullman Company treated its porters with disrespect. That porters tended to be better off than most black workers did not change the fact that company managers had created and institutionalized a system of employment bias that gouged and grated African Americans. Pullman's white managers and workers discriminated against the black porters for personal and corporate gain, and they

A porter prepares a bed on the "Capitol Limited" from Washington, D.C., to Chicago, 1942, Library of Congress, Prints & Photographs Division, Office of War Information, Overseas Picture Division—Washington Division, photograph by Jack Delano, LC-USW3-000050-D.

constantly implied to the company's black workers that they were inferior and deserved no more than they received.

Pullman porters faced several basic forms of employment discrimination. They received far less money than whites did for comparable work. The average porter made $60 per month. The salary of a white conductor was $120. Porters were expected to supplement their wages with tips from customers. Tips were also the key to controlling black workers on the palace cars. No porter would dare to get out of line, no matter how badly a white patron treated him, for fear of losing that tip. Porters were expected to arrive five hours before their shift to prepare the train for departure. If no passengers boarded the Pullman car when the train left, the porters were still required to stay on the train until it reached its destination in the hopes that customers would be present for the return ride. Since there were no passengers, the porters received no tips. This practice was known as the *deadhead*. Porters frequently had to work back-to-back shifts on trains, on what was called the *double out*, without a rest period and sometimes at a lower rate of pay. On trips where the conductor was absent, the porter filled in, but earned only an extra $12 a month for this "in charge" work, far short of what a conductor would earn. In general, porters had atrocious working conditions. They rarely had time to rest, as management expected them to work around the clock. In any case, there were few places to sit and catch one's breath. Stealing a couple hours of sleep was also difficult. Frequently porters slept on tables or among the suitcases in the baggage car. The final major insult that Pullman porters endured was the omnipresent company spy. The incognito "spotter" checked up on the porter's work by running fingers along windowsills looking for dust or by asking for a shoeshine to see if the porter had the proper equipment. Incidentally, porters had to purchase all their cleaning supplies, including their shoeshine wax and rags. Pullman porters disliked the spotters more than anything else, because managers took the spotters' word without question and docked pay without hesitation. If a customer or a conductor or a spotter was a bigot, a porter could be in serious trouble. As a longtime Pullman porter, L. C. Richie, said, "any kind of punishment that they wanted to give you they'd give you during those days. Those were rough days, before the union."[3]

There had been attempts to form a porters' union before A. Philip Randolph entered the scene. Fed up with the mistreatment, black workers had formed labor organizations in 1909, 1910, 1913, and 1918. Each time, their efforts failed. However, the 1918 organizational drive had been different from the others. During the World War I, President Wilson's treasury secretary and wartime railroad czar William Gibbs McAdoo, who also became the president's

*Alfred MacMillan, Pullman porter resting in the men's washroom aboard the "Capitol Limited" bound for Chicago, Illinois, Library of Congress, Prints & Photographs Division, Office of War Information, Overseas Picture Division—Washington Division, photograph by Jack Delano, LC-USW3-000056-D.*

son-in-law, ordered that railroad workers be allowed to form unions and bargain collectively. McAdoo acted primarily out of concern for the uninterrupted movement of war materials and soldiers. The "Big Four" independent railroad unions—the Brotherhood of Engineers, the Order of Railroad Conductors and Brakemen, the Brotherhood of Firemen and Enginemen, and the Brotherhood of Railway Trainmen—jumped at the chance to increase their membership and power. Sensing their moment, black porters formed the Brotherhood of Sleeping Car Porters Protective Union. However, the union disappeared with the end of the war. Another union, the all-black Pullman Porters and Maids Protective Association (PPMPA), met a similar fate. This time, however, the Pullman Company decided to fight fire with fire. It established a rival company union, known as the Employee Representation Plan (ERP). The company allowed the PPMPA to continue, but it was weak, ineffectual, and offered only the most basic benefits to members such as limited medical and life insurance. Seemingly the ERP had the power to fight for better wages and working conditions. In truth, the company union had no power. It was a sop and an instrument of corporate welfare, an invention of the 1920s to quell worker dissatisfaction by offering workers a company-led employee organization, often along with relatively small wage and benefits increases.

When black porters became upset and verged on organizing a new union, the leaders of the ERP always called a meeting, listened to grievances, and at times secured minor concessions. Pullman's corporate welfare also worked to improve the company's image in the black community, making public complaints seem impolite, uncouth, and uncivil. Although the Pullman Company had lost some of its public esteem in the aftermath of the 1894 strike, it had repaired its image, at least in the black community, by funding hospitals and nursery schools, especially in northern cities such as Chicago. Additionally, the Pullman Company gave money to black churches and newspapers. Pullman's leaders were also careful to sound sympathetic to the plight of black Americans. For example, Pullman chairman of the board Robert Todd Lincoln acknowledged that the company paid low salaries to porters and that the custom of tipping bothered him. The porters themselves had mixed feelings about the company. Some, like Ashley Totten, felt that the time had come for change. It was time for the porters to challenge Pullman as well as the ERP. It was not a case of biting the hand that fed them but rather seeking to shake that hand as equals.

Although Randolph was the perfect choice to lead a new union movement among the porters, he had never been a porter. This was an asset; he had no connection to the company. Pullman company officials could not put pressure on him. Pullman managers had frequently discouraged and undermined the efforts of workers to form independent unions. Company officials employed dozens of spies, or stool pigeons, who reported quickly if any new organizing started. Sometimes managers fired pro-union porters, and at other times they hired thugs to bully them. Often, if the company learned that a pro-union porter had just purchased new furniture, a company official would telephone and ask how the porter planned to afford the payments if he were unemployed. Such intimidation tactics sometimes worked, but they did not stop the push for a new union. Yet, the threat of retribution initially forced Randolph to operate in secret until the first general public meeting of the new Brotherhood of Sleeping Car Porters.

Randolph had paved the way for this meeting by calling attention to the problems of Pullman porters in the July and August 1925 issues of the *Messenger*. In mid-August 1925, Randolph announced a meeting for August 25. The gathering took place in the large auditorium of the Imperial Lodge of Elks on 129th Street in Harlem. Randolph spent considerable time planning the momentous occasion, and with his new cadre of friends made several important decisions. First, he was clear about the name of the new union: the International Brotherhood of Sleeping Car Porters and Maids (BSCP). In the beginning, the BSCP was dedicated to organizing black men as well as women workers on Pullman cars. In 1929, however, the union dropped "maids" from its name, and it was always a brotherhood, a kind of labor fraternity just like the other major railroad unions. When asked decades later why he chose the word "brotherhood," Randolph responded that he used the word consciously: "The purpose was to get the men convinced of the fact that they were brothers and have a common interest, each one, in helping to make it possible for all porters to have a better life."[4] The second decision that Randolph made was to downplay his socialist beliefs. Although he never renounced his political philosophy, he did finally realize that his firebrand political rhetoric might impede the creation of a socialist vanguard of young people who could foster radical social and political change. Moreover, he understood that espousing such a doctrine might scare off porters. Thus he promised he "wouldn't talk to the men too much about Socialism."[5] Finally, he decided that he would have to accept some aspects of black culture without question. As much as it may have bothered him, the BSCP's first meeting was to begin with a prayer. Randolph, of course, did not lead the invocation.

As Randolph approached the podium to address the porters for the first time, he sensed the somber tension. He had to convince the five hundred skeptical porters attending the meeting to risk their lives and livelihoods for a union, for a brotherhood. He had to overcome their sense that it was futile to fight a powerful corporation like the Pullman Company. Randolph's plan to win over the crowd was first to promise changes in their working lives. He then persuaded them that he was the person who could deliver. The bread-and-butter issues were plain enough. Randolph said that once Pullman recognized the BSCP, the ERP would disband and along with it the practice of tipping. Porters would receive full wages, a 240-hour work month—that is, ten hours a day for six days—compensation for deadheading, the elimination of doubling out, and conductor's pay for conductor's work.

As he looked at the crowd, he could see that he still had their attention. Now came the hard part. How could this street socialist, this avowed atheist, lead a movement to beat the Pullman Company? He paused and then said: "I've spent my life . . . studying the economic and social history of our group from the days of slavery onward, and I've come to the conclusion that it is not enough to build churches. . . . You have to take that responsibility upon your own shoulders, building something on which you can depend, and not depend on the Pullman Company . . . you can't expect a Pullman conductor to take the responsibility upon himself to fight for you," he told them. The message was clear: they had to fight a powerful employer to improve their working conditions and pay.[6]

Randolph's words hit home. The porters were behind him. Now, Randolph tried to reassure them about the uncertain future, urging them to stick together despite any intimidation and despite the presence of labor spies or "stool pigeons," as Randolph called them. Years later, Randolph still remembered the laughs that that comment sparked. Randolph was not scared about company informants and neither were the porters. "I can only tell you that I will stand on my character, my history which has been made here in New York, trying to advance interests of black people."[7] That sealed the deal. After the meeting, hundreds of porters signed up to join the BSCP. The next day two hundred more porters arrived at the *Messenger*'s office and pledged to the union. Randolph and the porters were on their way. They would learn, however, that getting started was the easiest part of a twelve-year odyssey.

The first order of business for the new Brotherhood of Sleeping Car Porters was to build a treasury. Here Randolph's old connections paid off. In late 1925, Randolph appealed to his supporters on the board of the Garland Fund, which had donated previously to the *Messenger*. Again, the liberal philanthropist organization provided a grant of $10,000. The BSCP was off and running. The next step was to open several Brotherhood branches, or *locals*, across the country. In October 1925, Randolph left New York City for an organizational tour of Chicago, St. Louis, and Oakland. These cities' chapters along with New York, Atlanta, and Detroit, became the backbone of the

BSCP. The most important city, however, was Chicago, Pullman's hometown. The person whom Randolph had to see was Milton Price Webster, the porters' unofficial leader in the city. Although Randolph and Webster quickly became friends and colleagues in the Brotherhood, they could not have been more different. Like Chandler Owen, Randolph's previous collaborator, Webster seemed to adhere to a different set of personal rules. Whereas Randolph was tall, elegant, and charming, Webster was big, stout, and rough. Randolph never appeared without his suit; Webster never appeared without his half-chewed cigar. Randolph used his skillful oratory to build up his followers and the movement. Webster often used his voice to tear down his opponents. Randolph inspired selfless activism, while Webster inspired fear. When speaking on the same platform, Webster usually went first followed by Randolph. The former riled up the crowd and the latter bowled them over, motivating the audience with his Shakespearean oratory.

Born in 1887, two years before Randolph, Webster grew up in Clarksville, Tennessee, a city forty-five miles northwest of Nashville. When Webster was

*Leaders of the Brotherhood of Sleeping Car Porters. Randolph is center and Milton P. Webster is to his left, ca. 1930s, Library of Congress, Prints & Photographs Division, A. Philip Randolph Papers, LC-USZ62-104208.*

a young boy, his father moved the family to Chicago. According to the family story, they had been chased north by white racists in Clarksville. Largely self-educated, Webster had intellectual limits but understood politics and people very well. Tremendously charismatic, but stern and forceful, he was no pushover. Furthermore, Webster was a union man. For twenty years, he had worked as a Pullman porter, until the company fired him when he organized the Railroad Men's Benevolent Association. Afterward, he became something of a Republican Party hack, working as a court bailiff and running Chicago's all-black Sixth Ward. When he heard Randolph was coming to town, he was very skeptical. He had no desire to fight with the Pullman Company again, and he also had no reason to trust Randolph, a socialist radical who had never been a porter.

At the first BSCP meeting in Chicago on October 17, 1925, Randolph's audience must have made him feel a little nervous. The grumpy, cynical faces in the crowd probably made the meeting in Harlem seem more like a family reunion. Randolph, however, did not scare easily and gave an incredible speech. Although the audience as a group remained unconvinced, Webster was impressed, and immediately decided to join Randolph. Quickly the Chicago BSCP branch became one of the nation's most active. In 1927, the Chicago chapter claimed a membership of 1,150 porters and maids, second only to the New York City branch.

Initially, the Pullman Company looked upon the growth of the BSCP mostly as a nuisance that would disappear with the right kind of pressure. Managers did not feel that there was a need to smash the union as they had the American Railway Union in 1894. Rather, they employed a four-pronged approach. First, the company tried to intimidate the porters. When spotters and spies identified union workers, Pullman managers summarily fired them. Second, to divide the porters, Pullman officials hired Filipino, Chinese, and Mexican workers as replacements. Managers also made those who associated with the BSCP suffer. A case in point was Morris "Dad" Moore, a retired porter in his seventies, who provided off-duty porters in the Oakland area with safe, affordable lodging. Moore was pro-union to his core, and when he found out about the Brotherhood, he immediately began organizing his sleepy customers. When the company found out, Pullman officials canceled Moore's pension and announced that any porter staying with "Dad" Moore would be fired. These actions almost destroyed Moore and broke the Oakland BSCP. But in the end Moore and his local union were unstoppable.

In addition to dismissing and terrorizing porters and their helpers, the Pullman Company employed various public relations tactics to defeat the BSCP. Here the company's contacts in the black communities paid big dividends. In Chicago, for example, leading African American ministers publicly denounced the Brotherhood and Randolph. Reverend Archibald James Carey of the African Methodist Episcopal Church was a close friend of Edward F. Carry, Pullman's president in the 1920s. Carey not only funneled workers to the Company but also supported the company's economic, social, and political outlook. Once Randolph and the porters had established the BSCP, Carey ridiculed the Brotherhood from the pulpit and forbade the congregations in Chicago to allow A. Philip Randolph to speak before them. No matter how far Randolph had traveled away from his family's religion, being rebuffed so publicly by the AME must have soured his spirits just a little. But there were other public relations problems. The nation's major black newspapers, such as the *Chicago Defender* and *St. Louis Argus*, which had supported the Pullman Company before the union's creation, continued to do so, attacking the BSCP, seemingly day after day, issue after issue.

Pullman's third strategy to destroy the BSCP involved the ERP. In January 1926, the porter representatives of the Employee Representation Plan called for a meeting in Chicago. The small assembly discussed the company's offer to improve working conditions, including a $5 per month raise. The minimum salary for porters increased from $67.50 to $72.50 per month. At the time, the national average for a railroad worker was $140 per month. Although the Pullman Company's proposition marked a meager advance, the loyal porters who attended the conference lauded the offer. After thanking the company for its fairness, W. A. Hill, a porter from Cincinnati, insisted that the pay raise also helped to discredit radicalism, meaning of course Randolph and the Brotherhood. Ten months later, working through the ERP, the Pullman Company mandated the end to the pernicious practice of calling porters "George," although patrons frequently continued the practice.

Finally, to stop the BSCP, the Pullman Company launched various personal attacks against Randolph. One such incident became a central part of the Brotherhood's lore, although it may be more fiction than fact. The Pullman Company allegedly sent Randolph a blank, signed check with instructions to write in any amount. There was no need to provide more direction. Randolph knew that to sign it meant to sign the Brotherhood's death warrant. When buying him off failed, the Company settled on a strong-arm tactic. In early 1926, Randolph traveled to Chicago to meet with Webster. When Randolph got off the train, Chicago police immediately arrested him. There were no charges, but the company wanted to acquire photographs of Randolph in handcuffs, being booked, and behind bars, to discredit him later. Fortunately, Webster heard about the arrest. Because he was a bailiff, he was able to intervene and secure Randolph's release. Although the Pullman

Company continued to use dirty tricks to foil the BSCP, in the end, they used legal loopholes to ensnare Randolph and the Brotherhood within the federal government's bureaucratic labor relations machinery.

In 1926, just one year after the formation of the Brotherhood of Sleeping Car Porters, the federal government enacted the Railway Labor Act, which provided for the "prompt disposition" of all disputes between railroad carriers and their employees. Both sides had to mediate any disagreements about wages, rules, and working conditions. For Randolph and the BSCP, the Railway Labor Act was the means to their victory, or so they thought. The rules seemed simple enough. The law dictated that in order to become the authorized bargaining unit for the Pullman porters, Randolph had to write a letter to the company president, E. G. Carry, requesting a meeting. He did so, but waited in vain for a reply from Carry. The BSCP leader then took the next step according to the law: he informed the U.S. Board of Mediation that a dispute existed between the BSCP and the Pullman Company. The Mediation Board selected former Kentucky governor Edward P. Morrow to head the investigation. The BSCP tapped labor lawyer Donald P. Richberg to represent its interests. The problem, both then and now, was that good lawyers cost money, and Richberg was an excellent one. Fortunately, Randolph was able to secure yet another $10,000 grant from the Garland Fund. The infusion of cash was vital, because Randolph's traditional sources of income—the *Messenger* and his wife Lucille—were evaporating quickly: the magazine was teetering on bankruptcy and his wife's salon had closed. The money also allowed the BSCP to expand its organization in advance of Morrow's hearing on the labor dispute. By December 1926, the Brotherhood claimed a membership of 5,763, or roughly 53 percent of all Pullman porters, enough to demand a vote to determine who could represent the porters, the Brotherhood, or the ERP.

Rather quickly, the Pullman managers' strategy became clear. They would stall as long as they could to see if the porters' resolve would crumble. By mid-1927, the BSCP leaders' fears were coming true. Porters were not renewing their dues with the union. It was at this point that Randolph made his first mistake. In June, he wrote a letter to Pullman president E. G. Carry to show the BSCP's good faith to negotiate. Because they did not expect the letter, Pullman managers viewed it skeptically. To them, it suggested that Randolph had lost confidence in the union's ability to win. In other words, the company's strategy was working, and the BSCP was beginning to crack. Thus, rather than open the way for negotiations, Randolph's letter closed the door.

Soon after Randolph's failed attempt to negotiate, Mediation Board investigator Morrow concluded that there was no possibility of a settlement and that the Mediation Board had exhausted its efforts under the law. It was a crushing blow both to the process of organizing Pullman porters and to the leadership of the BSCP. Randolph's enemies pounced on the defeat. Editors at the *St. Louis Argus* criticized Randolph for promising so much and delivering so little. Randolph brushed off the condemnation and tried to revive his campaign by filing a petition with the federal government's Interstate Commerce Commission to investigate the practice of tipping on Pullman cars and determine if the Pullman Company should raise porters' wages. When that move also failed, Randolph decided to use the last weapon the union had left, a strike.

The black community and its newspapers met with skepticism the announcement that the BSCP would hold a strike vote. Of course, papers like the *St. Louis Argus* offered little support. Significantly, Randolph's friends were not lining up behind the union. The influential but unpredictable editor of the *Pittsburgh Courier*, Robert L. Vann, had been a strong BSCP backer from the beginning. But after the Mediation Board's decision and the call for a strike, his support waned. In April 1928, Vann and Randolph met secretly in Pittsburgh. Unbeknownst to Randolph, Pullman officials had been working with Vann, and they got him to offer the BSCP's leader a deal: the Pullman Company would agree to recognize the union if Randolph resigned. Moreover, Vann let Randolph know that he would be paid handsomely if he would only desert the union. As Vann explained, the company would never deal with a socialist. So, he would have to step aside for any final negotiations.

Although shocked that his friend had turned his coat and betrayed him, Randolph took the offer seriously and sought Milton Webster's advice. After consulting with Webster, Randolph wired Vann that he would resign, after Pullman recognized the BSCP as its bargaining agent for the porters. That, however, was not the deal. Vann told Randolph that he had to resign first. Having reached an insurmountable impasse, the secret negotiations broke down. At issue was whether Randolph was seriously considering Vann's proposal. Clearly, Pullman managers had contacted Vann and changed his mind about the BSCP. Perhaps Pullman operatives had offered to help Vann financially if he would help them rid the BSCP of Randolph. In any case, Randolph could not be bought. Angered, Vann responded by criticizing Randolph in his newspaper. Undeterred, the BSCP strike vote went forth, and by the end of May 1928, the porters had spoken. Six thousand—out of 10,000—Pullman porters had voted to walk off the trains, unless the company settled with the union.

With the tally of the strike vote in hand, Randolph again contacted the federal Mediation Board in hopes of getting Edward Morrow to engage in emergency negotiations. Morrow first talked with Randolph and then spoke with Pullman officials. In these discussions, his true stripes became apparent. Morrow reaffirmed the Pullman Company's view that the BSCP was not prepared to strike. Randolph and the Brotherhood did not know about these discussions between the Mediation Board and Pullman, but their effect was devastating. The board refused to mediate an emergency negotiation session between Pullman and the BSCP. There was nothing left to do other than go through with the strike.

To prepare the Brotherhood, Randolph took a trip out west, stopping at various BSCP chapters. When he arrived in St. Louis to see Ashley Totten, he found out quickly how serious the porters were. He met Totten in the basement of a building operated by an African American businessman. Totten had amassed shotguns, clubs, knives, and ammunition. Randolph was horrified, but Totten was resolute. He was not going to let Pullman bring in strikebreakers as company managers had in 1894. Seeing Totten may have sparked the first thoughts in Randolph, a devout pacifist, that the strike should not go forward. On that long train ride back to New York City, he must have begun to harbor serious doubts about the strike. When he returned to his Harlem office, there was a message waiting for him from William Green, president of the American Federation of Labor (AFL). In 1926, Green and Randolph had talked extensively about the possibility of the BSCP's joining the AFL, which was an umbrella labor organization that supported local unions in their fight to negotiate with employers and establish common union policies and practices. When Randolph and Webster had approached him about a charter, Green had been sympathetic, explaining that the all-black Brotherhood was welcome, but that the Hotel and Restaurant Employees' Alliance had claimed jurisdiction over them. In other words, to join the AFL, the BSCP would have to become part of the hotel workers' union. This prospect was unappealing because the hotel workers' union was a racist organization and planned to put the porters into a separate and segregated local. Not surprisingly, the BSCP rejected the offer. At this juncture, the BSCP did not join the AFL, but the two leaders remained cordial, and Green often offered Randolph advice. In fact, when he heard about the proposed BSCP strike, Green told Randolph to call it off. Green explained that the Pullman Company was simply too large and powerful for such a small, weak union to fight successfully. Green feared that the result of the Brotherhood's struggle would be the end of the porters' union.

It is fair to question Green's motives. The American Federation of Labor was not dedicated to black civil rights. Although at the organization's founding the AFL leaders had declared themselves proponents of interracial unionism, the AFL's fifty-year track record proved otherwise. Unlike the AFL's immediate predecessor, the Knights of Labor, the federation's unions tended to be all-white organizations. Until the late 1890s, the federation's leadership had fought against trade unions that barred black members. For example, in 1890, the AFL denied the International Association of Machinists an application for admission on the grounds that it discriminated against African Americans. But by 1900, such commitment to racial equality had disappeared as the AFL decided rather than exclude unions that barred blacks, it would prefer to organize all unions, regardless of racist practices, under its aegis. By the time Randolph applied for admission into the AFL in 1926, the federation had changed little. A handful of its affiliated unions, like the Railway and Steamship Clerks Union, blatantly denied membership to blacks. Others, like the Boilermakers, made black workers join segregated and separate locals, which had no control over working conditions. The federation also created special unions for black workers. These organizations were notoriously weak. Thus, the AFL's record on race relations begs the question: why did Green call Randolph? Similarly, why would Randolph take Green seriously and even discuss joining the AFL?

In fact, Green felt sympathy and solidarity with Randolph and the BSCP. But there was little Green could do to transform the AFL overnight. He promised to take the porters' cause before the AFL's executive council, but he doubted that he could secure enough funds to see the strike to the end. Still, he promised to talk more about making the BSCP the first all-black, independent union to affiliate with the AFL. For the moment, that was little solace. Randolph had to listen to that voice inside him that said something was wrong. Without substantial financial backing, the Brotherhood was in no position to launch a successful strike. The BSCP had only a paltry strike fund, and since it was not a member of the AFL it could not expect much external support. Randolph listened to Green, thanked him for his opinion, and immediately contacted Webster in Chicago. Although doing so would be embarrassing and damaging to their movement, they agreed to call off the strike. As Webster wrote in a letter to the BSCP's branches, if the porters launched a strike, the federal Mediation Board would not interfere; this meant that the BSCP would alone face the Pullman Company, which had millions of dollars. Webster concluded that if the strike had come to pass, the BSCP would have walked into a trap and the union would have been crippled or would have ceased to exist.

Although it was probably the right thing to do, canceling the strike was exceedingly dangerous. Everyone was angry: the porters as well as Randolph's enemies. Communists in the labor movement, including former socialist friends, attacked Randolph as a sellout to Green, the AFL, and perhaps the Pullman Company. Since the Bolshevik Revolution in Russia in 1917, American communists and socialists had developed a deep rift between them. The main communist labor organization for African Americans, the American Negro Labor Congress (ANLC), which had been established in 1925, had long taken a dim view of Randolph, and in return Randolph had fired back in the pages of the *Messenger*. Now that Randolph was vulnerable, the ANLC pushed him down lower. Randolph instructed Webster to organize the porters to fight back.

The communists were undeterred and remained a thorn in Randolph's side for decades to come. But for the moment, they were the least of his problems. In January 1928, his brother James died of diphtheria. It was a tragic and shocking loss. Randolph was brokenhearted. James was just a few credits short of completing his bachelor's degree at New York's City College, and he would have been the first, and only, member of Randolph's family to earn a college degree. Following a path set by W.E. B. Du Bois, James had planned to apply to the University of Berlin's graduate school to study mathematics and languages. But all that was gone in an instant. Forlorn, Randolph told a friend after the funeral that he could not bear to live in a world without his brother. He remarked to a friend that he would rather fight a dozen Pullman companies than live without James.

Canceling the strike cost the union greatly. Between 1928 and 1932, as the Great Depression had started to grip the nation, the Brotherhood lost 90 percent of its membership. Many porters felt that the BSCP no longer represented their interests. In addition, rail traffic itself was down, as fewer Americans had the money to travel. The Pullman Company believed that it had no other recourse than to lay off hundreds of workers. In 1932, at the BSCP's lowest point, there were only 771 members. The union was broke. It could not even pay its organizers. Those who remained, including Randolph and Webster, worked for free. During the doldrums of the early years, O. W. Bynum, a porter who had been fired for supporting the union, took a train to Harlem to help Ashley Totten at the BSCP office. It was Christmas, and no one was willing to donate his or her scarce Depression-era savings to the union. Bynum and Totten failed to sign up new porters or find new supporters. Worse, they did not even have enough money for Bynum's return trip home. The two spent that Christmas alone in the cold BSCP office. They spread out newspapers for comfort and slept on Randolph's big, hard, wooden desk. This was the most trying time of Randolph's life. Not only was the BSCP on the verge of disintegration but his magazine, the *Messenger*, died an ignominious death. By the time Randolph stopped publishing it, the journal had gone from being "the only radical magazine published by Negroes" to being the staid, pleasant, and bourgeois "new opinion of the New Negro." Although Randolph eventually started another magazine, *Black Worker*, his literary days were all but over.

As had been the case before, Randolph was down but not out. He and the BSCP had several things going for them. There was Randolph's abiding and incorruptible faith in his work and in his union. He could have left the Brotherhood around this point. In 1933, the newly elected mayor of New York City, Fiorello LaGuardia, offered him a $7,000-a-year municipal position. The mayor was worried about his friend who looked as though he were down to his last dollar. Randolph refused. As he told fellow porters, he already had a job.

Rather than let things go to pieces, Randolph always dressed for work in a three-piece suit. From 1928 to 1932, his suits became frayed and dirtied. But he still respected his career and his porters. It was Randolph's spirit that kept the union alive and his lieutenants on board. Randolph was the hero, and those who remained in the BSCP supported him to the last. Many influential porters such as C. L. Dellums, head of the BSCP Oakland branch, felt that the union might not survive and that their noble efforts had failed. At this point, despite his own apprehensions, Randolph rallied the troops. At a meeting of BSCP leaders, Randolph exhorted them not to give up their faith in the union. He made them all hold hands and pledge their loyalty to the Brotherhood. In terms of material possessions, the BSCP was very poor. But, the remaining members of the Brotherhood still had spirit and trust in one another and the union.

The BSCP survived these difficult years in part because of the aid of several groups. In 1928, Randolph created a new organization, the Women's Economic Council (WEC), which was made up of porters' wives and female relatives. Through various fundraising activities, the WEC was able to keep the Brotherhood alive in much the same way as Lucille had sustained Randolph in the early years. Over time, the WEC became quite large and influential. In 1938, the council, led by Halena Wilson of Chicago, transformed itself into the Ladies Auxiliary of International Brotherhood of Sleeping Car Porters. Increasingly the BSCP looked like any other trade union in the United States. Like so many AFL unions, the Brotherhood was sex segregated. In general, black women did not belong to the union, but rather to the union auxiliary. Ideally, the porters wanted their wives and sisters to join the auxiliary to support them and their union activities, and essentially, they believed that women's roles should be confined to domestic concerns. Initially, the porters had organized Pullman maids. In 1929, in a move that illustrated what some might call their sexist views, the porters dropped "maids" from their masthead and from the union. The BSCP was an organization devoted to empowering black men economically, politically, and socially. To do that, they wanted to foster independent, assertive, and robust men, and they wanted their wives and sisters to be respectable "ladies."

In addition to the WEC, the American Federation of Labor aided the BSCP. In 1934, Randolph once again sought a charter with the AFL. Such an affiliation had clear economic benefits such as access to strike funds. But there was another reason for belonging to the federation. For good or for ill, the AFL represented the interests of most organized workers in the United States, and the BSCP needed to tap into that sense of political clout and social status. But without AFL funds or the federation's support, the Brotherhood was likely to disappear. In 1929, when Randolph again approached Green, the AFL leader offered an independent, but not a full-fledged, charter, which was what the BSCP wanted and needed. Nonetheless, joining the AFL was an important, positive step. One cannot underestimate how important the support and encouragement of the AFL and the Women's Economic Council were. These two organizations propped up Randolph, Webster, and their miniscule group until it could grow again.

This opportunity for growth came in the midst of America's greatest economic and political challenge, the Great Depression. Although devastating, the economic collapse gave rise to a new kind of leader and a new kind of federal government. Unlike his predecessors, President Franklin D. Roosevelt and his liberal wing of the Democratic Party sought to change the ways in which the federal government interacted in the economy and with average people. New Dealers firmly believed that the government could help ordinary Americans recover their lives while fixing the stagnant, dormant economy. A centerpiece of the New Deal was the new model of labor relations. President Roosevelt wanted workers to organize into unions, bargain collectively with employers, and fashion employment contracts that would allow workers to support themselves and their families. The business community was generally skeptical about New Deal labor relations. However, there were rewards for them. In addition to peaceful relationships with their workers, employers could expect workers with growing incomes to spend more money on the products they were making.

The key pieces of legislation that put New Deal ideas about workers into law were the National Industrial Recovery Act (1933) with its famous Section 7(a). The law guaranteed workers the right to organize and bargain collectively. Additionally, it created the National Labor Relations Board (NLRB) to monitor union elections and ensure that employers acted fairly.

When the U.S. Supreme Court ruled the NIRA unconstitutional in 1935, Democrats in Congress quickly passed the 1935 National Labor Relations Act (also known as the Wagner Act), which kept New Deal labor relations alive.

Randolph and the BSCP could have appealed to the new NLRB for help with the Pullman Company. Instead, they worked through legal appeals to the 1934 Railway Labor Act. In 1934, Congress amended the 1926 Railway Labor Act to specifically cover sleeping car and other nonoperating train workers. After President Roosevelt signed the law it was perfectly legal for porters to join the Brotherhood of Sleeping Car Porters. Conversely, it was illegal for the Pullman Company to fire workers for joining the union. Moreover, the BSCP now could ask for an election to select bargaining representatives. An election was essential because there were three unions vying for the porters' dues. The Brotherhood was challenged by the Order of Sleeping Car Porters (OSCP), another AFL union of black porters based in Canada, and the Pullman Porters' Protective Association (PPPA), the labor organization that the company had set up. To defeat its AFL rival, Randolph and Webster went to the federation's 1934 convention. To Randolph's chagrin and Webster's great dismay, Green sided with the OSCP, not the Brotherhood. By rejecting Green's wishes and walking away from the convention, Randolph and the BSCP technically left the AFL for a brief period. However, it did not matter. In June 1935, the National Mediation Board held an election to determine which union, the BSCP or the PPPA, would have the bargaining rights of Pullman porters. The OSCP was not a factor largely because it had failed to make many inroads into the United States. The Brotherhood won in a landslide, capturing 71 percent of the eligible vote and coming out on top in 26 of the 28 cities holding elections.

But Pullman's president E. G. Carry refused to abide by the election results. Despite the law, he did not want to deal with Randolph. The company pursued two strategies to defeat the BSCP. First, it helped launch a Supreme Court challenge to the 1934 Railway Labor Act. This legal challenge was part of a broader big business counterattack on the New Deal. While Carry went after the Railway Labor Act, his colleagues sought to eliminate the Wagner Act. Second, Carry and other like-minded employers threw their considerable political weight and fortunes behind President Roosevelt's 1936 presidential election rivals, the Republican Alfred Landon and the Liberty League candidate William Lemke. Carry and his friends lost on both accounts, and Roosevelt won by a wide margin in 1936. Moreover on April 1, 1937, the U.S. Supreme Court ruled against the Pullman Company. On August 25, 1937, twelve years to the day after its birth, the Brotherhood of

Sleeping Car Porters signed a contract agreement with the Pullman Company that not only bestowed recognition on the union but also reduced monthly work hours and increased wages.

Although Randolph never achieved all his dreams, he did cause a revolution in the labor movement. His union was the first all-black union to sign a deal with a major American corporation. The porters had endured a twelve-year odyssey of classical proportions. At the end of it, Randolph emerged on top. At the Brotherhood's victory party, which he sponsored at City Hall, New York City mayor Fiorello La Guardia called Randolph the foremost progressive labor leader in America. And the Brotherhood itself was now a powerful force in the black community and the nation generally. In just four short years, all Americans would learn just how powerful Randolph and his Brotherhood truly were. They became the advanced guard for reforming American race relations and improving the conditions of the working class.

## Notes

1. "Reminiscences of A. Philip Randolph," 7 August 1972, Columbia University Oral History Research Office, 235. Hereinafter, Randolph oral history.
2. Jack Santino, *Miles of Smiles, Years of Struggle: Stories of Black Pullman Porters* (Urbana: University of Illinois Press, 1991). 8.
3. Santino, *Miles of Smiles*, 23.
4. Randolph oral history, 242.
5. Randolph oral history, 275.
6. Randolph oral history, 235–36.
7. Randolph oral history, 237.

CHAPTER THREE

# When Negroes Don't March: A. Philip Randolph and the Power of Protest Politics During World War II

> Hence, let the Negro masses speak! Let the Negro masses march! Let the Negro masses fight!
>
> —A. Philip Randolph, 1941[1]

By launching the Brotherhood of Sleeping Car Porters, Randolph had indeed built what he considered a vanguard to transform American life. The Brotherhood was not just a porters' union. It shared Randolph's vision of equality and opportunity for all workers regardless of race. And the union was dedicated, willing, and strong, growing by leaps and bounds after Randolph signed the collective bargaining agreement with the Pullman Company. The start of World War II in 1939 provided an additional spark for membership. The defense mobilization caused an incredible rise in American rail traffic, and of course porters benefited greatly as passenger trains became longer and more ubiquitous. At the same time, as war clouds grew darker for the United States, all porters—old and new members—looked to Randolph for leadership on wartime union and political issues. He led them to challenge the racial status quo and thereby transformed race relations in America.

By the time of World War II, Randolph was not merely the porters' indisputable leader, but he had also become a hero of the African American working class. He was a rising star among race leaders. However, many of them looked down on Randolph as an upstart. In reality, Randolph was quite different from Walter White, fair-skinned head of the National Association for the Advancement of Colored People, and Lester Granger, the quiet and refined president of the National Urban League. Despite his rich baritone, somewhat haughty, Shakespearean voice, Randolph had no pretense to be anything but a leader of black workers. At the same time, he was not the second coming of Marcus Garvey. Randolph's tactics were clear, concrete, and practical. During World War II, he used all his leadership skills and charisma to advance civil rights by blending both union and racial activism. Rallying the black working class to his cause, Randolph established himself as the nation's preeminent pioneer of nonviolent mass protest politics. The Brotherhood remained his base of operations. But the BSCP and Randolph were at the forefront of the civil rights movement. In the early 1940s, they pushed Americans to reform the social order and laid the foundations of modern America.

Even before World War II, Randolph labored mightily to bring the forces of the labor and the civil rights movements together to solve the longstanding troubles of African American workers in particular and all workers in general. In the mid-1930s, he was among a handful of relatively young black intellectuals and reformers such as Howard University political science professor Ralph J. Bunche, Bunche's friend and fellow civil rights activist John P. Davis, eminent sociologist E. Franklin Frazier, and economists Abram L. Harris and Robert C. Weaver, who united to improve the lives of black Americans suffering as a result of the Great Depression. The organization that they formed, the National Negro Congress (NNC), emerged from a 1935 conference at Howard University in Washington, D.C. Leading black politicians along with labor, civil rights, and community leaders had assembled to discuss the New Deal and its relationship with black America. Everyone present agreed that President Franklin D. Roosevelt had tried to help African Americans. Nevertheless, they believed that Roosevelt should provide more relief. Formally established the next year, the NNC was dedicated to expanding the New Deal for African Americans as well as eliminating racism and discrimination in American society.

The National Negro Congress was a racially integrated organization that initially welcomed all ideological views. Specifically, the leadership encouraged unity on the American political Left. The 1930s were an unusual time where old political adversaries such as communists and socialists temporarily set aside their differences and joined together for common causes such as the promotion of civil rights and the opposition to fascism. Such "popular front" activities, as contemporaries called them, made it possible for the selection of A. Philip Randolph as the NNC's first president. Randolph, a socialist, led a congress whose membership included moderates belonging to groups like the NAACP as well as radicals with ties to the Communist Party. For three years, under Randolph's leadership, this odd collection of activists in the NNC engaged in several battles to assist African Americans. For example, the congress aided the Scottsboro "Boys," a group of nine young, unemployed African American men unjustly accused and convicted in Alabama for raping two white women. Although the NNC's work for the Scottsboro Nine did not result in the men's immediate release, the efforts did help the young men's long struggle to gain justice.

The popular front alliance within the NNC did not last long. In 1939, after the Soviet Union and Nazi Germany signed a nonaggression pact, communists inside the NNC—and outside it too—dropped their near-religious crusade against fascism. The rest of the NNC felt betrayed by the communists' changing allegiances. In turn, the communists revived their denunciation of socialists and liberals who did not join them. The infighting reached a peak at the 1940 NNC convention when Randolph finally broke his ties with the congress and its communist members. For years, he had defended the NNC's communists from public attacks. For example, he stood by John P. Davis, who had strong connections with the Communist Party, when Walter White of the NAACP accused Davis of trying to poach on the association's antilynching activities. Randolph had also tried hard to convince those like Milton Webster, who had always remained skeptical of the congress, to lend a hand with the organization. Furthermore, Randolph publicly denied charges that the NNC was a communist-front organization. To Randolph, the fact that the NNC and the Communist Party shared goals was evidence that some communist ideas were sound. The NNC's communists soon made Randolph wish that he had never made those claims.

At the NNC's third meeting in 1940, the communists revealed themselves and the firm grip that they held over the congress. Much to Randolph's surprise they proposed two resolutions that reflected the politics of the radical Left rather than the conciliatory attitudes of the popular front. The first resolution condemned President Franklin D. Roosevelt's foreign policy, which had been critical of the Soviet Union's nonaggression pact with Nazi Germany. As Randolph's allies tried to defend President Roosevelt, the resolution's authors and supporters booed them off the stage. The second resolution called for direct cooperation with industrial labor leader John L. Lewis and his Congress of Industrial Organizations (CIO). The CIO had broken away from the American Federation of Labor in 1935 after fighting over the best way to organize workers as well as over issues of racial and sex discrimination. Importantly, the CIO drew heavy support from those on the Left, particularly communists. However, Randolph also opposed this resolution because it aligned the NNC with a particular kind of politics and a particular kind of labor organizing. He wanted the NNC to remain neutral about the rift between the AFL and CIO. But Randolph lost this battle. In fact, both resolutions passed with large majorities. The raucous convention made two things clear to Randolph. First, he had lost control of the congress to the communists. Second, the NNC had become an anti-Roosevelt, pro-CIO, and pro-communist organization. Randolph was none of these things, and immediately following the 1940 meeting he left the NNC for good. The congress itself limped along without Randolph, disappearing by the 1950s, although it did help propel the cause of African American civil rights. For Randolph, his experiences with the NNC left a bitter taste. From that point on, he shied away from working with those on the radical Left, and for a time he avoided working with sympathetic whites out of a fear that such collaborations would invite communist infiltration.

Randolph's unceremonious exit from the NNC was both a personal and a professional setback replete with a dose of public humiliation. But never one to second-guess his decisions or to take a break from his political ambitions, Randolph launched his next endeavor, the creation of equal employment opportunities in America's defense industries. To do so, he relied heavily on the Brotherhood of Sleeping Car Porters, not the NNC. In fact, by 1940, the original purpose of the NNC was quickly fading. As war engulfed Europe, the defense emergency, as President Roosevelt called it, rapidly eclipsed the Great Depression as the nation's primary concern. For many civil rights activists, this transformation meant that the most salient political issue of the day was no longer equal participation in the New Deal but equality on the home and battlefronts of World War II. Once again, it was A. Philip Randolph who led the charge. With the Brotherhood of Sleeping Car Porters at his side, Randolph fought to make the "arsenal of democracy" much more democratic.

In 1939, as President Roosevelt took the first steps to put the United States on a war footing, the American economy had yet to emerge fully from the Great Depression. In fact, unemployment that year was a staggering 17 percent. For blacks, the rate was well over 20 percent. It was still the case that the economic depression hurt African Americans more than any other group. In 1930, for example, blacks had made up 9.7 percent of the American population. Yet they had made up over 16 percent of those on public relief. Not only could black workers not find jobs but New Deal opportunities were few and far between. The old saying still rang true: blacks were the first fired and the last hired for any jobs, even government work. As employment opportunities became plentiful during the defense emergency between late 1939 and late 1941, blacks still found it difficult to find work. Mainly white workers were benefiting from the upswing in the production of military goods and services. In fact, they were leaving New Deal work programs in droves and landing good-paying union and nonunion jobs in factories, making planes, ships, tanks, and guns. The history of the Civilian Conservation Corps (CCC) provides a telling example. The CCC was a popular and effective work relief program that focused on environmental conservation and internal improvements. From the corps' inception in 1933, it discriminated against blacks. Although the legislation that created the CCC specifically outlawed employment discrimination on account of race, color, and creed, the CCC's leaders, particularly the agency's chief administrator Robert Fechner, ignored that part of the law. At first, the corps employed no African Americans. Vocal protests from civil rights groups and some New Dealers resulted in the token placement of a few black men. By 1934, Georgia had enrolled 178 in the program. Alabama had 778 black corpsmen. Mississippi established the poorest record. Although blacks amounted to 50 percent of the state's population, blacks comprised only 1.7 percent of the total number of men working in the state's CCC camps. Moreover, all corps programs were segregated. The situation did not change until 1940 when good-paying defense work lured white corpsmen away. To make up for the loss in manpower, the CCC finally enrolled more black workers. Yet, this advance within the CCC was short lived. Citing the availability of defense-related employment, Congress decided to kill the Civilian Conservation Corps as well as other New Deal work programs in 1942.

Thus, although white workers easily found jobs in war industries, blacks were not so lucky. Increasingly the New Deal was unable to help them, and most American industrialists had no use for them. Take the story of Louise Boyd, an African American woman living in Cincinnati, Ohio. Shortly after Japan's devastating attack on Pearl Harbor, she read an advertisement in the *Cincinnati Post* calling for women to apply for war factory work. Those interested were to sign up at the local United States Employment Service (USES) office, which handled all manpower issues in the city. Boyd dutifully showed up and began to fill out the required paperwork. All that she needed was a high school education and the ability to meet a few physical specifications: a height of five feet two inches, a physically fit body, and an age of at least seventeen. Boyd fit all the qualifications but the government official rejected her. "I met all the requirements but one," she explained, "my face is black." When she complained to a USES official, he told her that he was "sorry we have nothing for colored."[2] Boyd's experience was not exceptional.

Like so many Americans, after the Pearl Harbor attack, Thomas Doram wanted to do something to help his country. In late December 1941, an opportunity appeared. The twenty-nine-year-old Doram took a new war job at the massive California Shipyards (Calship) in Los Angeles. He started at the very bottom as a janitor. But the pay was decent, and Doram saw the possibility for promotion. Three months later, Doram got his chance. He joined Local 92 of the International Brotherhood of Boilermakers, Iron Ship Builders, and Helpers of America, received his union book and insurance policy, and became a shipyard helper. Despite the desperate need for workers on the docks, this job advance was quite unusual. The Boilermakers did not allow African Americans into their union. But Doram, who was light skinned, could pass for white and thus had passed his union initiation ceremony. Within another three weeks, Doram was promoted to a welder position on the production line. In January 1943, keeping his racial identity a secret, he applied for yet another promotion and became an instructor training white welders. Shortly thereafter his troubles began.

Youlen Dixon, Doram's immediate supervisor, suspected that his welding instructor was in fact African American. At first, Dixon planned to force Doram to quit his job: he called Doram names and threatened him physically. When that did not work, Dixon tried to get him fired by complaining about him to the foreman. Doram pleaded with the foreman not to fire him, pointing out his excellent work. Sympathetic, the foreman put him on the night shift hoping that Dixon, who had an earlier shift, would ignore him. Unfortunately, Dixon refused to let matters drop. On June 29, 1943, soon after Doram started his shift, Dixon and his friend Paul Morris cornered him in the bowels of an unfinished Liberty ship. A fight ensued. Doram bested his attackers, who had come armed with wrenches and knives. Yet, despite the fact that the potentially fatal attack was unprovoked and motivated by racism, Doram, and not Dixon or Morris, paid the price for this confrontation. Calship fired him the next day for behavior unbecoming of an employee, and the Boilermakers Local 92 kicked him out of the union for being black. Adding insult to injury, soon after, police officers arrested him for assault. Doram was tried, convicted, and sentenced to thirty days in jail.

The arsenal of democracy's military arm was as unwelcoming to African Americans as was its industrial arm. Racial segregation and discrimination in the military were nothing new in the 1940s. But by the early twentieth century, racial discrimination in the armed forces became even more rigid and more bureaucratic. Following World War I, the Army War College issued a report that claimed that African Americans were not physically qualified for combat duty and were inherently inferior and subservient. Thus, the report falsely asserted that black soldiers were capable of performing only the most menial jobs in the military. By World War II, these ideas had become ingrained in military policies. Regardless of qualifications, experiences, or rank of African American soldiers, the military frequently discriminated against them, as did related organizations like the Red Cross and United Service Organizations (USO). Black recruits did the hot and heavy work in the various military branches. For example, all black sailors worked in the kitchens of the U.S. Navy. The other branches segregated their African American personnel, and the Marine Corps and Army Air Corps barred them. Furthermore, the army denied black soldiers the use of base stores and recreational areas. Black officers could not even use the officers' clubs. Moreover, military officials stonewalled initial attempts to change the conditions of black soldiers. For example, when pressed on the issue of equality in the military, Undersecretary of War Robert Patterson responded that the army was not a sociological laboratory for experiments to improve the lives of American minorities. Patterson claimed that any program or policy to help blacks would destroy military morale and discipline. In other words, according to those who ran the military, maintaining racial discrimination was essential to keeping a strong military.

African Americans were outraged at the persistence of white supremacy in the armed forces. A. Philip Randolph's disdain for the U.S. military and for war itself was well known long before he began to protest racism in the services. In September 1940, the BSCP held its annual meeting at the Harlem YMCA. At the top of the agenda was a frank discussion of discrimination in the army, navy, and air corps. The convention passed a resolution calling on President Roosevelt to end discrimination in the military. Randolph knew that the Brotherhood's message would reach the president, for he had made sure that Roosevelt's top adviser on racial matters, his wife Eleanor, attended the meeting. The First Lady, who spoke after the resolution passed unanimously, promised to do her part in improving the situation once she returned to the White House.

Eleanor kept her word. Just ten days after the BSCP gathering, President Roosevelt called a meeting of America's top race leaders and the president's military advisers for September 27, 1940. Eleanor Roosevelt, who had pushed for the conference, had urged her husband to act immediately to eliminate discrimination in the military and in defense industries. The president led the session. Two of Roosevelt's top military leaders were there: Undersecretary of War Robert Patterson and Secretary of the Navy Frank Knox as well as Randolph, the NAACP's Walter White, and the National Urban League's T. Arnold Hill.

Randolph had been to the White House once before. In 1925 he went with a group led by the radical civil rights activist Monroe Trotter to ask President Calvin Coolidge to work for federal legislation outlawing lynching.

Of course, Coolidge gave no such support for a federal antilynching law. To say the least, Randolph had higher expectations of his first visit with President Roosevelt. Although his work with the NNC had served to highlight the New Deal's shortcomings, he understood that the Roosevelt administration had done more for blacks than any other administration since the days of Lincoln. Despite Randolph's high hopes, however, the encounter did not go very well.

Roosevelt and his military advisers appeared swayed, convinced that serious reform was necessary. By the meeting's end, there was agreement that officials of the army, navy, Marines, and Coast Guard would place African Americans in combat as well as supply roles. Moreover, the military officials promised to place black officers in command positions. The president also assured Randolph, the NAACP's White, and the NUL's Hill that aviation training would be offered to black pilots. Finally, Roosevelt, Patterson, and Knox promised to uphold the antidiscrimination section of the 1940 Selective Service and Training Act, which forbade discrimination against any person on account of race or color. But two weeks later, White House Press Secretary Stephen Early issued a statement reporting that at the September 27 meeting Roosevelt had discussed the War Department's policy with respect to African Americans and that the policy of the War Department was not to mix black and white enlisted personnel in the same regimental organizations. The White House press release stated further that after conferring with Randolph, Hill, and White, Roosevelt had approved the deal. Although technically correct—Roosevelt did approve a segregation policy some time after meeting with Randolph, White, and Hill—the public memo implied that one was linked to the other. Randolph, White, and Hill had been hoodwinked and were justifiably infuriated. Early's press release made it appear as if the trio had approved the military's racist policies. And, despite vehement denunciations from White, Randolph, and Hill, the president refused to issue a retraction or a restatement.

The meeting with Roosevelt was not a total failure. In late 1940, the War Department announced that it had begun training black pilots at Tuskegee, Alabama, one-time home of Booker T. Washington. Within a year, the army was training all-black ground crews and an all-black fighter unit, the Ninety-ninth Pursuit Squadron. Navy officials made plans for a training station for black sailors. The subsequent installation, Camp Robert Smalls, was connected to the gigantic Great Lakes Naval Station near Chicago, Illinois. It was, however, a segregated facility. Finally, the president, in conjunction with his military brass, made three high-level appointments. First, Colonel Benjamin O. Davis, Jr., received the command of the all-black Tuskegee-based 332nd Fighter Group, which was deployed to the Mediterranean in 1943. Second, Colonel Campbell Johnson became the executive assistant to the Selective Service director, General Lewis B. Hershey. Third, President Roosevelt appointed William H. Hastie—a federal judge, dean of Howard University's law school, and civil rights leader—as a civilian aide to Secretary of War Henry L. Stimson.

During the war, African Americans served valiantly in the armed services. Three million registered for the draft. At the war's peak in 1944, over 700,000 were in the U.S. Army; 165,000 were in the U.S. Navy; 17,000 were in the U.S. Marines; and 5,000 were in the Coast Guard. Furthermore, hundreds of black women joined the armed forces as nurses and as members of the Women's Army Corps (WACs). In all, the one million African American men and women in uniform constituted about 6 percent of the entire American military force. By the war's end, four Liberty ships had black captains who led integrated crews. Eighteen ships were named for prominent African Americans including the *Booker T. Washington*, the *Frederick Douglass*, and the *Robert L. Vann*. Following the war, both the army and the navy made strides toward integration. Nonetheless, the treatment of black soldiers was far less than equal. Draft boards rejected blacks at more than twice the rate they rejected whites. Those in the service were segregated and abused, including the celebrated sailor Dorie Miller. Born to Texas sharecroppers in 1919, Miller enlisted in the U.S. Navy in 1938 and was relegated to kitchen duty. When the Japanese attacked Pearl Harbor, Miller was aboard the USS *Arizona*. When the bombs and bullets began to rain down, he was below deck. Leaving his post, he ran above deck, saving his captain's life in the process. There he noticed a vacant machine gun nest. He jumped in and began to fire the gun, shooting down a handful of Japanese airplanes. On May 27, 1942, military officials recognized Miller's courage by bestowing on him the prestigious Navy Cross. Then they sent him back to mess duty without a promotion. There were thousands of similar, sometimes worse, stories of racial injustice. In a Kentucky railway station, white police beat three black women in uniform for not leaving a white waiting room. The U.S. Army limited the number of black nurses with a quota system and allowed them to treat only German prisoners. The practice continued throughout the war despite an acute shortage of nurses and the vehement protests of Mabel K. Staupers, who before the war had been active in the National Council of Negro Women and had led the National Association of Colored Graduate Nurses. In fact, German prisoners of war were often treated better than black soldiers.

Wearing the uniform did not change life for African Americans all that much. To the rest of white America, they were still black, still second-class citizens. Seemingly, there was little anyone could do. In January 1943, the War Department's civilian aide on "Negro affairs," William H. Hastie, resigned in frustration and disgust. He had labored for over two years to end the military's discriminatory practices without result and left his post bitterly, denouncing the armed services' biased policies and harmful practices. Hastie was not the only one who was disaffected. For example, in 1943, New York City's draft board sent a postcard to Malcolm Little. Even at age eighteen, Little, who later adopted the name Malcolm X, was a radical. Dutifully, he appeared before the board. Detroit Red, his Harlem nickname in the 1940s, had made public statements that he was frantic to join the *Japanese* army so that he could get a gun and kill whites in the South. The draft board immediately sent him to the army psychiatrist, and later the board rejected him.

Although Detroit Red's actions might have been provocative and extreme, they illustrate the low level of African American morale during much of the war. From the most senior government officials like Hastie to the street hustlers like Little, there was a growing sense among black Americans that the war was not a war for democracy. After military conflict broke out in Europe in 1939, black columnist George Schuyler wrote that it was a white man's war. The NAACP's magazine, the *Crisis*, agreed, stating that the editors felt sorry for the nations involved in the growing global conflict, but that they also wanted democracy in the United States.

President Roosevelt viewed black protests with concern. As early as 1939, J. Edgar Hoover, the head of the Federal Bureau of Investigation, had been keeping tabs on pro-Axis, anti-American sentiment in the United States. Always on the lookout for foreign-inspired subversives, Hoover soon convinced Roosevelt to authorize a vast intelligence-gathering operation in America's black communities. This investigation became the basis of the secret FBI report entitled *The Survey of Racial Conditions in the United States* (*RACON*).

Hoover discovered what everyone already knew: only some African Americans supported the American war effort wholeheartedly while many more were disillusioned with race relations in the United States and displayed little patriotism. However, instead of outlining the roots of black discontent, Hoover's investigators blamed Axis spies and propaganda, American left-wing radicals like A. Philip Randolph and the black communist James W. Ford, and the black press. FBI director Hoover put great pressure on Roosevelt and his attorney general, Francis Biddle, to use sedition laws to arrest and incarcerate those who spoke up against the federal government. President Roosevelt refused to do that, and black dissent continued unabated during the war. But the president was not interested in taking any positive steps to address the complaints of African Americans who wanted to serve their country. A. Philip Randolph saw it as his job to make President Roosevelt listen and act.

In 1940, a few months after Randolph's White House visit, he and his most trusted collaborator, Milton Webster, boarded a train in Washington, D.C. Their plan was to visit the southern Brotherhood divisions. As the train entered Virginia, both men, who were rarely silent about anything, were sitting pensively. Webster later blamed his reticence on bad memories of the South. He and his father had escaped white supremacists bent on mayhem and perhaps murder. Randolph's mind was on the present and the future. Finally, he leaned over to his friend and broke the silence. He suggested that instead of holding a fruitless conference with President Roosevelt, the two should lead a march of 10,000 blacks down Pennsylvania Avenue to protest discrimination in the armed forces and in the defense factories. With some trepidation, Webster agreed to help.

As they traveled throughout the South, Randolph and Webster used their BSCP brothers as sounding boards for the idea of a march on Washington. In some areas, the reception was quite cool. In Savannah, Georgia, the local BSCP arranged a meeting to discuss the proposed march. Randolph laid his idea out and no one spoke. As Webster explained, the idea scared everyone to death. In much of the South—and the North too—a white lynch mob could form quickly if blacks exercised their political rights. Undeterred, Randolph kept talking and making plans. On January 15, 1941, he issued a press release to the national papers. Drawing inspiration from his socialist past, Randolph called on the African American masses to use the power of their numbers to pressure the federal government to enforce their rights as citizens to work and to fight for their country.

The idea of a march on Washington represented an advance in Randolph's political philosophy. It melded his socialist desire to rally the masses for social and political change with his newfound faith in Gandhian nonviolent protest. Indian nationalist Mohandas K. Gandhi first used *satyagraha*, passive resistance and civil disobedience, in his civil rights battles in South Africa and in India. Like Gandhi, Randolph also believed that the truth of any injustice was strong enough to change the situation. The trick was getting the message out to the public and getting people to listen. This was the genius of the march. It had the potential of not only capturing the hearts and minds of the black masses but also the ears of political leaders in the White House and on Capitol Hill.

Randolph was not the first to attempt such a march. Three important precedents were the march of Coxey's Army in 1894, the 1913 Great Suffrage

March, and the Bonus Army march of 1932. Randolph was too young to remember Coxey's march. In the midst of the economic depression of the 1890s, Ohio native Jacob Sechler Coxey decided that the U.S. Congress had to increase the amount of legal tender currency and create federal work projects to restore the economy. To deliver this message, Coxey organized a battalion of unemployed workers to become a "living petition" for their idea. The march took place on April 30, 1894. Coxey mobilized only 500 marchers, all of whom were arrested before reaching Capitol Hill. Nonetheless, the march inspired similar attempts in the late 1890s and became a historical touchstone for others. Randolph probably did remember the women's suffrage march in 1913; led by Alice Paul and Lucy Burns, this was a pinnacle event for suffragists. These radical two reformers rallied nearly 10,000 women who demanded the right to vote in a march that showcased over two dozen floats, ten bands, and six golden chariots. The 1932 Bonus Army march was also quite memorable. Over 15,000 World War I veterans staged a march on Washington and demanded that Congress authorize immediate cash payments of their military service bonuses, which had been granted in the 1920s. President Herbert Hoover and the leaders of Congress rejected the request and sent federal troops to disperse the marchers. Randolph was building upon tradition, but he also wanted to avoid the violence and failures of previous marches.

To increase the odds that his march would be successful, Randolph quickly enlisted the support of other major civil rights leaders. Many race leaders had already called for decisive federal action to eliminate discrimination in the defense effort. In May 1940, Howard University political science professor Rayford W. Logan and *Pittsburgh Courier* editor Robert L. Vann had formed the Committee on Participation of Negroes in the National Defense Program. The NAACP also began to focus on the issue. On January 26, 1941—roughly ten days after Randolph's first call to march—the NAACP staged protest meetings in twenty-three states to "celebrate" National Defense Day. Association members picketed defense factories and government offices to raise awareness of the problems of blacks who wanted to serve their country. Soon after, Randolph approached the National Urban League's Lester Granger, scholar Rayford Logan, Walter White, and a dozen other civil rights and labor leaders. Setting their rivalries aside for the moment, all agreed to help Randolph. In particular, Walter White was especially encouraging, providing advice, money, and moral support. Thus, the March on Washington Movement (MOWM) was born in the spirit of racial unity against a common foe: discrimination in the industrial and military mobilizations.[3]

The organization was very different from the National Negro Congress, Randolph's previous civil rights engagement. Like the Brotherhood of Sleeping Car Porters, the MOWM was all black. Although some black civil rights leaders such as the NAACP's Walter White and Charles H. Houston (who was also Howard University's law school dean) complained, Randolph excluded whites from the MOWM to limit the influence of the Communist Party, most of whom were white. The Communists hoped that African Americans would join them, and not their rivals. Aside from internal political battles on the American Left, there was another reason why Randolph segregated the MOWM. Like other African American leaders and writers such as W. E. B. Du Bois, Ralph Bunche, Abram Harris, and Chester Hime, who had come of age at the turn of the twentieth century, Randolph was fundamentally committed to improving the lives of black workers. Based on his experiences with the National Negro Congress, Randolph also believed that the black working class had to fight on its own, with the occasional help of sympathetic whites, to advance their causes. Such thoughts were extraordinarily radical, perhaps revolutionary, at that time.

Once assembled, the MOWM announced its intention to march. In March 1941, Randolph publicly reissued the call, telling potential marchers that they possessed the power necessary to effect change that would affect the entire nation, reminding them that nothing could happen without their collective pressure. Although some reporters took note of this announcement, there was no indication that anyone in the White House noticed. Thus, on May 10, 1941, and then again on May 29, Randolph sent President Roosevelt letters complaining that black workers and soldiers had been discriminated against while trying to get jobs in defense industries and join the military. Therefore, he told the president, he was mobilizing ten to fifty thousand blacks for a march on Washington. Randolph set July 1, 1941, as the date for the protest, which he called the March on Washington for Jobs and Equal Participation in National Defense. The assembly planned to walk down Pennsylvania Avenue and end up at a mass rally at the Lincoln Memorial because of the monument's historical symbolism in the struggle for African American civil rights.

These May announcements were newsworthy. Major newspapers, such as the *New York Times*, carried word of Randolph's correspondence with the White House. Soon, those critical of Randolph began voicing opposition to the march. His old foes jumped at the chance to attack him. Even though Robert Vann had died in 1940, the *Pittsburgh Courier* carried on Vann's feud with Randolph and wrote that the march was a "crackpot proposal." "We doubt," the newspaper's editors opined, "if these people have plans to handle 5,000 visiting Negroes, let alone 50,000."[4] The paper also ran editorials criticizing Randolph. One even likened Randolph to Hitler, inciting the masses to outrageous actions. After June 22, 1941—the day when the Nazis launched an ill-advised invasion of the Soviet Union—American communists added their voice to the naysayers. Although mass protests had been a typical communist strategy, party officials frowned on the idea, fearing that it would somehow disrupt American support for the Soviet Union in the war against the Nazis. The White House also wanted to stop the march. President Roosevelt told one of his most trusted aides that the march would certainly stir up racial hatred if it took place. For the sake of wartime unity and for the sake of the defense mobilization, the president tried to prevent Randolph's march.

President Roosevelt took both public and private action to pressure Randolph into calling off the march. To placate African Americans, particularly Randolph, Roosevelt had Sidney Hillman, a longtime labor union leader and codirector of Roosevelt's industrial mobilization agency, the Office of Production Management (OPM), issue a press release concerning the administration's successful efforts to lessen and limit racial discrimination in employment. The release, which was carried in major newspapers such as the *New York Times*, explained that since 1940 the OPM's Hillman and his assistant in racial matters, Robert C. Weaver, had made progress in creating jobs for black workers in defense factories. Citing cases such as Chester, Pennsylvania's, Sun Shipbuilding and Dry Dock Company, where 10 percent of the yard's workers were black, Hillman promised that additional job opportunities were quickly becoming available. The message was clear: there was no need for a march on Washington. Be patient, the White House was saying, and jobs would be available for black Americans.

Privately, President Roosevelt put some heavy pressure on Randolph to relent. Roosevelt had his wife, who was an NAACP member and had many friends in the black community, send Randolph a discouraging letter. On June 10, the First Lady wrote that she had talked it over with her husband and felt that Randolph was making a grave mistake. Her fear was that the march would set back the progress being made in the military and defense industries. She also thought it could poison American politics and foster a wider conservative backlash in Congress. Finally, she reminded Randolph that she was deeply supportive of black civil rights and that marches were sometimes necessary, but this one would be unwise.

President Roosevelt thought that his political maneuverings had a great chance of succeeding. But Randolph was immune to this political pressure. By the spring of 1941, plans for the D.C. march were progressing. Supported by black newspapers such as the *Chicago Defender* and the *Amsterdam News* along with thousands of BSCP porters, who brought word of the march to black communities throughout the nation, the MOWM was indeed gathering thousands of supporters. The March on Washington Movement's branch offices in Harlem, Brooklyn, Chicago, Detroit, and Los Angeles had already scheduled preliminary local marches to build enthusiasm for the national one in Washington, D.C. The regional offices had also collected thousands of dollars through various fundraisers and donations to help defray the costs of transportation and lodging in the nation's capital. By June 1941, the MOWM had hired buses and chartered special trains. The march was becoming a reality.

Finally, on June 18, 1941, President Roosevelt called A. Philip Randolph and Walter White to the White House to discuss the proposed march. In addition to the two African American leaders, Secretary of War Henry Stimson, his assistant Robert Patterson, Secretary of the Navy Frank Knox, and various other government officials and influence peddlers including New York City mayor Fiorello La Guardia were present. Although Roosevelt was the first president to install a secret recording device in the Oval Office, unfortunately no one recorded this meeting. Rather, what remains are the reminiscences of Randolph and White. After brief pleasantries, the group got down to business. Randolph again stated the problem: employers and military officials were denying African Americans the right to work and the right to serve in the military. The president then asked what he could do. Randolph suggested that an executive order banning discrimination would be a concrete positive step. Initially Roosevelt guffawed at the idea. One wonders if at this point Randolph recalled his previous meeting with President Coolidge, who had easily rebuffed the demands of black leaders. Roosevelt was trying to do the same, albeit in a more pleasant manner. Randolph, however, was not going to be silenced or to settle for anything less than what he wanted. Instead of caving, he pressed further and stated that 100,000 black workers would march. This was ten times the number in the MOWM's original call. Roosevelt turned to Walter White, who had been silent until that point. He asked White how many were going to march. White supported Randolph and coolly said 100,000. After several more minutes of negotiation, the president finally agreed to an executive order and offered another idea: a new federal agency to enforce the ban on discrimination in war industries. In return for the executive order, Randolph and the MOWM had to cancel the march. Randolph had won, but now the work began in earnest.

The job of writing what became Executive Order 8802 fell to a young administration official and future civil rights leader named Joseph L. Rauh, Jr. President Roosevelt signed the executive order on June 25, 1941. It became a milestone in civil rights history. Executive Order 8802 established a nondiscrimination employment policy for the federal government during the war years. In it, the president explained that because "available and needed workers [had] been barred from employment in industries engaged in defense production solely because of consideration of race, creed, color, or national origin," it was now national policy that "there shall be no discrimination in the employment of workers in defense industries or Government because of race, creed, color, or national origin."[5] The order also created the Fair Employment Practice Committee (FEPC) to investigate and redress complaints of job bias.

The FEPC was initially a blue-ribbon committee with high profile appointees that in fact did very little. The president appointed the heads of both major national labor organizations, William Green, president of the American Federation of Labor, and Philip Murray, president of the Congress of Industrial Organizations. To represent employers, Roosevelt chose Radio Corporation of America president David Sarnoff. Roosevelt also wanted Randolph to serve on the FEPC. Randolph knew that he would be in trouble for canceling the march. Adding a government appointment to his deal with President Roosevelt—or even seriously considering it as Du Bois had—might destroy his reputation forever. Rather, Randolph negotiated for the president to appoint his right-hand man on the BSCP and MOWM, Milton P. Webster. Roosevelt did not completely trust Webster, who was a Republican operative in Chicago. To balance Webster's appointment, the president also appointed Earl Dickerson, a black politician in the Chicago's Democratic Party machine.

Many civil rights leaders praised Executive Order 8802 and the formation of the Fair Employment Practice Committee. Randolph immediately became canonized as "Saint Philip of the Pullman Porters."[6] In rapid succession black leaders bestowed significant honors on him. In 1941, he received the NAACP's Spingarn Award, which normally went to exemplary black scientists, writers, and artists. But in 1941, according to the award committee, there was no one more deserving or influential than A. Philip Randolph. That same year, Howard University conferred on him an honorary doctorate. Smaller, but no less meaningful, was the recognition of the Schomburg Center and the *Chicago Defender*, which put Randolph on their yearly honor rolls. Praise for Executive Order 8802 was no less lavish. Many heralded it as the Second Emancipation Proclamation.

There were those, however, who belittled Executive Order 8802 and ridiculed Randolph. Black newspapers with close ties to the Republican Party dismissed Roosevelt's groundbreaking action. The *Cleveland Gazette*'s editors called the order "teethless," and many papers such as the *Philadelphia Tribune* and the *Baltimore Afro-American* agreed. Other African Americans were angered that the president had addressed only one of the MOWM's complaints—the order did not deal with discrimination in the military. To activists such as journalist Roi Ottley, Randolph had actually lost prestige among blacks because the executive order was a mere public pronouncement and had no real value. Additionally, Ottley agreed with MOWM Youth Division leaders Bayard Rustin and Richard Parish, who repudiated the deal with President Roosevelt and demanded that the march proceed as planned. They wrote Randolph demanding that the MOWM "press forward with vigor to secure [African Americans'] full participation in American life."[7]

Randolph was resolute and unapologetic. Moreover, he did not explain exactly why he did not press the president on discrimination in the military. Perhaps he might have decided to stop while he was ahead. He might have believed that further concessions from the president were not possible, or the military officials present might have convinced him that further advances were in the offing without presidential action. Regardless, in a lengthy public letter, Randolph rebuffed his critics, saying that the MOWM had gained most of their objectives and that future advances were still possible. Moreover, he dismissed his harshest critics as youthful dilettantes, who had fallen prey to the communists.

As it turned out, Randolph's critics were wrong, at least about the president's efforts to stop unfair job bias. Executive Order 8802 was no mere public announcement designed to appease outraged African Americans. Likewise, the Fair Employment Practice Committee was no sop. Rather, the committee became one of the most controversial and influential of Roosevelt's agencies. Although it was only an administrative body with no powers to subpoena, fine, or jail offenders, the FEPC became quite adept at using moral suasion as its main weapon for creating equal employment opportunities. In late summer 1941, the FEPC launched a wide-ranging investigation of job discrimination across the nation. It held several public hearings in New York, Chicago, Los Angeles, and Birmingham, Alabama. The committee's intention was to raise awareness of the problems that racist hiring practices caused and to cajole employers and union leaders to adopt democratic methods by calling them out in public. Such actions were without precedent and in Birmingham whites considered them revolutionary. White supremacists made death threats against the FEPC, specifically against Milton Webster and Earl Dickerson, the two African Americans on the committee. Undeterred, the FEPC exposed discrimination in defense employment in the Birmingham area and singled out the worst employers and unions, embarrassing them as unpatriotic and bad industrial soldiers in the arsenal of democracy.

The FEPC's actions outraged white supremacists and conservatives in both major political parties. Committee chairman Mark Ethridge had tried to smooth the ruffled feathers at the 1942 Birmingham hearing. In his opening statement, Ethridge boldly asserted that neither the FEPC nor any other power in the world could force the South to abandon segregation. His words did nothing to appease the FEPC's racist critics. Rather, they began to mobilize political pressure in Washington, D.C., to kill the committee. Moreover, Ethridge had shocked and discouraged the FEPC's supporters. How could the head of the first federal agency since the end of the Civil War designed to help African Americans make such a conservative statement? As MOWM president, Randolph knew he had to act fast to save the FEPC, not only from those who sought to maintain the racial status quo but also from the committee's inept leadership.

In the spring of 1942, the situation worsened for Randolph. In late May 1942, owing to political pressure from southern conservative forces in the Democratic Party, President Roosevelt transferred the Fair Employment Practice Committee, which had been a freestanding, independent White House agency, into the War Manpower Commission, the President's all-powerful wartime industrial mobilization agency. The FEPC was now subsumed under the leadership of the conservative midwesterner Paul V. McNutt. During a subsequent press conference, Roosevelt denied that he had hobbled his first and only civil rights committee. Everyone knew better. McNutt made it impossible for the FEPC to do its job, and by the late summer of 1942, the committee was defunct.

Randolph, the MOWM, and the BSCP came to the FEPC's rescue. On June 12, 1942, the March on Washington Movement staged massive "Save the FEPC" rallies in New York and Chicago. Randolph had also wanted a Washington, D.C., rally, but the White House denied his request for permission to gather at the Lincoln Memorial, explaining that the march was too controversial. In other words, government officials feared a race riot if blacks marched on Washington. Regardless, the rallies were extraordinarily successful. Thousands of African Americans filled the Chicago Coliseum and Madison Square Garden. Randolph, who strolled in with a parade of BSCP porters, attended the New York assembly. Unfortunately, so many speakers appeared that Randolph never got a chance to deliver his address to the crowd.

President Roosevelt got the message loud and clear. After a summer of additional "Save the FEPC" rallies in the Midwest and in Washington, D.C., Roosevelt rethought his position on fair employment. In the spring of 1943, the president issued a new antidiscrimination executive order. This one, number 9346, reaffirmed his first fair employment order and reestablished the Fair Employment Practice Committee as an independent agency, giving it more authority and more money to carry out its mission. For the remainder of its life until the FEPC was disbanded in 1946, the committee did groundbreaking work, fighting discrimination by major employers, unions, and the federal government. With limited resources and time, the FEPC by no means eradicated employment discrimination in America. However, it made significant accomplishments, and it demonstrated the great practicality of federal action to reduce employment discrimination. In other words, the reform and governmental activism that Randolph had secured worked. He had won again, although some in black America like the editors of the *Pittsburgh Courier* continued to dog him with criticism. Generally immune to such sniping, Randolph must have known that this was his shining moment. The wayward radical from Crescent City had become one of the most influential and powerful leaders in America, capable of making even the president of United States take action on the thorniest of all political issues.

In late 1943, not content to rest on his laurels, Randolph set about making his new political position permanent. In September, he helped establish a new organization, the National Council for a Permanent FEPC (NCPFEPC). As a wartime agency, President Roosevelt's FEPC was destined to survive only until the Allies beat the Axis. Randolph's new group planned to have the U.S. Congress make the FEPC permanent through new legislation. In some ways, the NCPFEPC and the March on Washington Movement resembled each other. Both promoted the work of the wartime FEPC. Both drew the same kinds of liberal and left-wing political supporters, although the National Council was an integrated group unlike the MOWM. And, both wanted the federal government to continue its work to eradicate employment discrimination. Unlike the MOWM, however, the NCPFEPC never quite took off. Whereas the MOWM had a broad leadership group, Randolph kept the National Council tightly under his control. The titular head of the organization was Reverend Dr. Allan Knight Chalmers, the conservative and politically well-connected pastor of the New York City Broadway Tabernacle Church. Such an ally was perhaps the perfect choice because it suggested that the group was not radical. To do the day-to-day work, Randolph tapped Anna Arnold Hedgeman, a former MOWM staffer, as executive secretary. Nonetheless, the NCPFEPC's small leadership cadre was not particularly successful either in building the organization or in achieving its goals.

As World War II approached its climax, all signs pointed to the very real possibility that the federal government would institute some sort of permanent fair employment practice commission. Owing to the work of the many civil rights organizations such as the NAACP, the National Urban League, and Randolph's two fair employment groups, the MOWM and the National Council, there was a groundswell of activity. In communities across the nation, fair employment practices had become a widely recognized and generally supported political issue. Local groups, including branches of the NCPFEPC, helped to fan the political flames by sponsoring "FEPC Sundays" at churches, "FEPC Dances," and "FEPC Rallies." The city of Philadelphia even celebrated an entire "FEPC Week." The idea of a permanent FEPC was not just the hobbyhorse of civil rights activists. By the mid-1940s, several notable conservative Americans, including Henry R. Luce, editor of *Time*, *Life*, and *Fortune* magazines; Eric Johnston, the former president of the United States Chamber of Commerce; and Nelson A. Rockefeller lent their names to the movement for a permanent FEPC. With support growing, Randolph felt the time was right to introduce legislation in the House of Representatives to establish a permanent FEPC. The NCPFEPC, however, failed to score a victory in the halls of Congress. Randolph underestimated the level of resistance by the so-called Conservative Coalition composed of southern Democrats and anti-New Deal Republicans. Since the late 1930s, they had limited and in some cases blocked President Roosevelt's agenda. After Roosevelt's death in April 1945, the ascendancy of this congressional coalition became finalized, and this spelled doom for all bills proposing a permanent FEPC. Like the MOWM, the NCPFEPC was dedicated to nonviolence ideals and sought peaceful but dramatic political reform. Some of Randolph's supporters, who had invested so much into making the March on Washington Movement successful, felt a little betrayed. But Randolph encouraged them to join his new organization. In any case, by the end of World War II, the MOWM was financially broke and drifting without a clear purpose since it had largely achieved its goals. In 1947, it finally disbanded, leaving just a small remnant of one of the most dynamic mass movements: the March Community Bookshop in Harlem, New York.

In the final analysis, Randolph's proposed 1941 march on Washington may be the most significant nonevent in American history. With the unprecedented successful use of nonviolent pressure politics, the March on Washington Movement captured some Americans' attention and forced whites—although haltingly and in a limited way—to begin to deal with a major legacy of slavery: the continued patterns of employment discrimination across the nation. It also catapulted A. Philip Randolph into the stratosphere of black leadership in America. He was now the principal deal maker and deal breaker. With masses of black workers behind him, he had positioned himself to launch an all-out assault on the structure of Jim Crow, which had created in reality two Americas: one white and relatively wealthy and one nonwhite and poor. Randolph had already identified the targets in his battle against American racism during the World War II. For the next twenty years of his life, he waged an uphill campaign to bring democracy to the American economy, to the American military, and to American life generally. Although Randolph changed as the times changed, he remained a true radical, never compromising his principles for quick gains or for personal profit. Unfortunately, the postwar battle against American racism was more complicated and laborious than he could have possibly imagined.

## Notes

1. A. Philip Randolph, "Let the Negro Masses Speak," *The Black Worker* 7, no. 3 (March 1941): 4.

2. *Cincinnati Post*, 3 March 1942.

3. The March on Washington Movement was originally known as the Negro March on Washington Committee. Randolph changed the name in 1942. For simplicity, I have used the group's final name.

4. "That March on Washington," *Pittsburgh Courier* (14 June 1941): 6.

5. "Executive Order 8802," *Federal Register* 6, no. 125 (27 June 1941): 4544.

6. Herbert Garfinkel, *When Negroes March: The March on Washington and the Organizational Politics for FEPC* (Glencoe, IL: Free Press, 1959), 62.

7. Garfinkel, *When Negroes March*, 67.

CHAPTER FOUR

# Unfinished Business: Randolph's Civil Rights Struggles During the Cold War

> I feel morally obligated to disturb and keep disturbed the conscience of Jim Crow America. In resisting the insult of Jim Crowism to the soul of black America, we are helping to save the soul of America. And let me add that I am opposed to Russian totalitarian communism and all its works. I consider it a menace to freedom.... But democracy and Christianity must be boldly and courageously applied for all men regardless of race, color, creed, or country.
>
> —A. Philip Randolph, 1948[1]

In April 1946, A. Philip Randolph turned sixty years old. Despite the wear and tear of decades of social and political activism, he showed no signs of slowing down. Rather, the next decade and a half were his most productive years. He was the titular leader of a vanguard of African American workers and several major organizations, including the Brotherhood of Sleeping Car Porters. From this position, Randolph sought to change American politics, eliminate discrimination in the armed forces and in employment, and reshape the labor movement. This ambitious agenda was essentially the unfinished business of the wartime civil rights movement. World War II was a watershed event that transformed the black freedom struggle. No longer was it a sideshow of the national political arena. Civil rights reform was at the center stage, and Randolph was no mere circus barker. He was the ringmaster, trying to get the attention of every unionist, every citizen, and every politician focused on building upon the wartime advances in American race relations and improving conditions for the black working class. To some extent, during the late 1940s and early 1950s, Randolph accomplished much of what he wanted. But these advances came at a personal and political cost. By 1960, a new group of brash young activists had emerged, and they had supplanted him. By the early Kennedy years, Randolph's powers were diminished as years of attacks from his opponents and his own weaknesses as a leader began to take their toll. Nonetheless, Randolph's Cold War years were pivotal and represented the pinnacle of his career.

The decades that followed World War II were extraordinarily contentious and dangerous. The guns and canons of the Allied armies had barely cooled when another world war seemed in the offing. The two world superpowers left standing after the conflict with the Axis powers, the United States and the Union of Soviet Socialist Republics (USSR), were making preparations to fight each other for global supremacy. That war in fact did not take place. Rather a prolonged "cold war" ensued, as the United States and the Soviet Union staged global diplomatic battles and waged war through surrogates to achieve their aims. This fifty-year conflict dramatically shaped not only American foreign but also domestic politics. As Randolph quickly learned, the postwar years were not just conservative but precarious and full of pitfalls. To move his agenda forward, he had to tailor his arguments and actions to meet the shifting political sands of the Cold War and the antiradical, red-baiting witch hunts on the home front. Randolph always had to be careful that his ideas and programs could not be construed or misconstrued as communist-inspired activities.

This situation was not wholly unfamiliar to him. In fact, Randolph had already lived through one "red scare." Following World War I, President Woodrow Wilson's attorney general A. Mitchell Palmer, along with his chief aide J. Edgar Hoover, had embarked on a nationwide campaign to arrest, imprison, and in some cases deport radicals belonging to various leftist political and labor organizations. The "fighting Quaker," as Mitchell was known, attacked such groups as the Industrial Workers of the World as well as political dissenters, like the world-renowned anarchists Emma Goldman and Alexander Berkman who were exiled to Russia. In all, over 2,700 suspected radicals were caught up in the Palmer Raids' dragnet. The Red Scare and the conservative Republican politics of the 1920s had their origins in World War I. The 1917 Espionage Act and 1918 Sedition Act had set the stage for what was to come. Randolph himself had been arrested on federal sedition charges and was branded one of the most dangerous radicals in America in 1918.

Like the red scare of 1919, the era that bears Senator Joseph P. McCarthy's name was born out of war. In the late 1930s, as President Franklin

D. Roosevelt made his first moves to mobilize the nation's defenses, he gave FBI chief J. Edgar Hoover the special assignment of tracking radical groups that opposed his presidency. Roosevelt had implied that Hoover should investigate mainly right-wing organizations such as the German American Bund, but Hoover took his mandate to include left-wing activists and institutions. Thus began decades of surveillance of individuals and groups that the federal government deemed subversive. Once again and not surprisingly, Randolph was on the FBI's watch list. On December 1, 1941—just months after the MOWM's leader had wrestled Executive Order 8802 from the president—Hoover signed a classified memorandum stating that Randolph should be imprisoned in the event of a national emergency. Radicals like him lived under a cloud of suspicion for the entire duration of World War II. In 1940, President Roosevelt signed the Alien Registration Act, commonly known as the Smith Act, which strengthened immigration and deportation laws, required the fingerprinting of all aliens in the United States, and made it illegal for anyone to advocate the overthrow or destruction of the federal government. The FBI used this latter section of the law to maintain its domestic surveillance during the war and after. Although Roosevelt did not use his office to attack radicals, his Democratic and Republican successors did.

Similarities aside, the two red scares were quite different. The one that started after World War II was more long lived and more culturally pervasive than its World War I counterpart. The Red Scare that began in the 1940s affected nearly all aspects of American society and politics. Moreover, despite the political repression, the McCarthy era afforded more opportunities for social change, even for socialists like A. Philip Randolph. During the Cold War, the Americans styled themselves as the torchbearers of democracy, freedom, and liberty, fighting the epic battle against the godless, communist, totalitarian Russians. Not surprisingly, evidence to the contrary was quite embarrassing and damaging, as it served as fodder for the Soviets' propaganda machine. It also provided a stark reminder to Americans that their nation was far from perfect. To try to make American ideals match American realities and to combat communist criticism of American democracy, politicians, particularly Cold War-era presidents, were often compelled to seek remedies for the social ills of the nation.

Perhaps nothing was more harmful to America's image abroad than the sorry state of its race relations. During the Cold War, there were numerous domestic and diplomatic racial incidents that not only shamed Americans but also created unique conditions for change. In February 1946, the U.S. Army discharged black soldier Isaac Woodard, who immediately traveled home to South Carolina. Arriving in uniform, Woodard was attacked by policemen who pulled him from a bus and jabbed nightsticks into his eyes, blinding him. Four months later in Monroe, Georgia, a white mob abducted two black veterans and their wives, drove them to the countryside, and executed them. Recording the crime scene, police noted that the assailants had shot sixty bullets into the victims' bodies. Tragic episodes like these along with the well-documented, omnipresent, daily discrimination against African Americans and other American minority groups revealed to the world the hypocrisies of American democracy. Civil rights activists strongly urged presidents from Harry S. Truman to Lyndon B. Johnson to act to correct these domestic injustices in part to uphold America's claim as the standard-bearer for human rights in the world.

Racial incidents involving foreign diplomats similarly pushed presidents toward reform. As foreign ambassadors discovered firsthand, the Soviets were indeed telling the truth about American race relations. Despite the advances of World War II, like the creation of the Fair Employment Practice Committee, most blacks, Hispanics, and Asians were essentially second-class citizens. Moreover, most of the American people treated great reform leaders like A. Philip Randolph with disdain. No one had to read the Soviet daily newspaper *Pravda* to learn about Jim Crow in America. All one had to do was get into an automobile and drive along an American interstate highway. For example, once the United Nations complex was built in New York City in 1949, African diplomats faced terrible humiliations when they had to travel to Washington, D.C., to visit with the president or his advisers. Along Maryland's Route 40, no restaurants served African Americans, let alone Africans. For years, no politician was willing to change this situation. But as the Cold War ideological battlegrounds moved to Africa, someone had to act. Still, few had the political will to act. Finally in the early 1960s, a reluctant President John F. Kennedy assented to a State Department plan to help end the indignities by helping to change Maryland's segregation laws. Initially, Kennedy had resisted this idea, instructing his State Department officials to tell the African ambassadors to fly instead of driving to the capital. But Kennedy finally realized that insulting African dignitaries who angrily returned to their home countries posed a great a risk to America's global strategy to defeat communism.

Thus Cold War politics, while at times stifling, could create openings for civil rights activists to challenge the racism in the United States. Appealing to Cold War ideals on human rights did indeed move some politicians to act. Thus, despite the dominance of political conservatives in the late 1940s and through the mid-1960s, there were opportunities for those dedicated to transforming American society. Randolph's vision for changing postwar America already began to crystallize during World War II, when the U.S. Supreme Court handed down a landmark decision in April 1944. In *Smith v. Allwright*, the justices ruled that the all-white Texas primary election was unconstitutional. For seven decades, conservative, lily-white Democrats had controlled Texas politics. By excluding African Americans from participating in the Democratic primary election, which for all intents and purposes was the Texas general election because the state had only one functioning political party, blacks were disenfranchised. The Court's ruling opened Texas to black voters for the first time since Reconstruction. Using his magazine *Black Worker* and working through BSCP representatives, A. Philip Randolph stridently argued that black Texans should register and vote in the elections in November 1944. He called for them to cast their ballots as an independent bloc, showing no loyalty to New Deal-supporting Democrats or the few Republicans in the state. Rather, he wanted African Americans to exercise their suffrage according to which candidates promised to do the most for African American communities and for civil rights reforms, particularly the federal bill to establish a permanent Fair Employment Practice Committee.

As the 1944 presidential election approached, Randolph repeated his demand for blacks to make the most of their vote, and he pressed for collective action on the part of black voters. He led the BSCP into a short-lived coalition of various civil rights groups, including the Southern Conference for Human Welfare and the NAACP black voter registration campaigns in the South and elsewhere. The high point of this wartime political offensive was the 1944 National Non-Partisan Political Conference. The BSCP sponsored this meeting, which took place in Milton Webster's hometown, Chicago. At this conference, Randolph criticized both major political parties. He claimed that there was no difference between the Republican and Democratic parties. He then outlined the political platform that should guide black voters. They should dispense with party allegiances and vote for those politicians who promised to support an FEPC law, an end to segregation and discrimination in the armed forces, and the enforcement of the Fourteenth and Fifteenth amendments to the U.S. Constitution.

As always, Randolph was hopeful that his words would win over even the most skeptical thinkers. But this time, black Americans outside the BSCP were not ready to follow Randolph's vanguard. During the 1944 election, African Americans behaved largely as they had in 1940 when those who could cast a ballot did so for liberal Democrats. Randolph was discouraged, believing that the Democrats had taken blacks for granted. The Democratic Party's 1944 platform had only the vaguest plank on civil rights:

> We believe that racial and religious minorities have the right to live, develop and vote equally with all citizens and share the rights that are guaranteed by our Constitution. Congress should exert its full constitutional powers to protect those rights.[2]

The Republicans, who nominated U.S. District Attorney Thomas E. Dewey for president, fashioned a much stronger party platform, which called for a permanent FEPC, federal legislation outlawing the poll tax and lynching, and an immediate investigation into discrimination in the armed forces. Still, the Republican Party's rhetoric and attempts to win back black voters had little effect. Blacks still voted for the party of Franklin and Eleanor Roosevelt.

Undeterred, Randolph did not give up his vision of an influential, independent, and well-respected African American electorate. Coming on the heels of the deadliest war that the world had ever known, Randolph felt that the time was right to form a new political party in the United States, one that had at its core an unshakable commitment to human dignity and civil rights. He envisioned a progressive, left-leaning party that would stand in opposition to the communists while carrying on the reform work of the 1930s. Implicit in this idea was the call for black voters to distance themselves from the Democrats and to act as an independent political vanguard. As the 1944 election had shown him, the Democratic Party was not yet ready to put strong civil rights at the center of the party's platform. Moreover, it was obvious to civil rights activists that newly installed president Harry S. Truman was not the race liberal that President Roosevelt had been.

There is no denying that by the time he became president, Truman was certainly not a rabid racist like many of his former senatorial colleagues such as Theodore G. Bilbo (Democrat of Mississippi) or Senator Richard B. Russell (Democrat of Georgia). In the late 1930s, Senator Truman (Democrat of Missouri) had agreed to an NAACP request to investigate racial discrimination in defense industry employment in Missouri, and he did support legislation— which never passed—to begin the process of integrating the armed forces. Yet, as president, Truman initially catered to the conservative wing of his Democratic Party, bowing to their wishes on racial issues. Nothing demonstrated this acquiescence better than Truman's relationship with the wartime FEPC. He consistently obstructed the committee's work, preventing it from conducting investigations and holding hearings. Then in late 1945 after a congressional coalition of conservative Republicans and Democrats significantly reduced its funding, President Truman issued Executive Order 9664, which basically terminated the FEPC. In the eyes of many on the Left—especially A. Philip Randolph—Truman's actions showed he was more a southern conservative than a New Dealer. Thus liberals and other Leftists began to search for someone to carry Roosevelt's torch. It was at this moment that Randolph began pressing for a new political party, whose main constituencies would be racial and ethnic minorities as well as disaffected workers, New Dealers, old-time Progressives, and of course socialists like Randolph.

In the spring of 1946, Randolph called together a group of unionists, farmers, and left-leaning, politically minded intellectuals who met in Chicago to form the National Education Committee for a New Party (NECNP). The committee was not a political party, but it set forth the guiding principles for a new party. The honorary chairman of the organization was the eighty-seven-year-old eminent American philosopher John Dewey. His selection to represent the NECNP was not mere coincidence. Unlike so many of his Progressive Era colleagues, Dewey had never relinquished his radical political beliefs. Dewey issued the same challenge as he had after World War I. In 1919, he had urged his reformist friends to recognize the opportunities that war created. In the progressive magazine *The New Republic*, he argued that the moment had come for Progressives and Socialists to dedicate themselves to using science for socially constructive purposes while attacking the inequality and the concentration of political power so that all Americans could enjoy freedom. Dewey thought that the moment for progressive social transformation had come again after World War II.

So did A. Philip Randolph, the committee's executive chairman. In the fall of 1946, Randolph arranged for the *Antioch Review* to publish the "Provisional Declaration of Principles" of the National Education Committee for a New Party. Intellectually, the long document was a blending of Socialist, Progressive, and New Deal thought, and it clearly showed the hallmarks of both Randolph and Dewey. The declaration began with a criticism of the existing political parties in the United States. Echoing Randolph's 1944 attack on the Democrats and Republicans, it stated that both parties had failed to meet the economic, social, and political challenges of the postwar period. Rather, a coalition of reactionary Democrats and Republicans had savagely destroyed Progressive measures designed to expand freedom and justice in the United States. To move the political reform agenda forward, the committee put forth a Wilsonesque fourteen-point domestic policy plan that included provisions for higher wages, an end of discrimination against labor unions, the expansion of social security, a rational use of natural resources, and, importantly, new protections for civil rights.

The declaration also carried a detailed plan for a "liberal economic democracy," which served as a pronouncement of beliefs and as a means to distance the committee from the communists. The group called for a limited socialization of industry. In other words, the declaration suggested that the federal government should take over the management of only certain segments of the economy. Although clearly a socialist idea, this was in fact a rejection of orthodox Marxism, which said that *all* major industries should be state owned and operated. The committee had socialist leanings but was decidedly anticommunist. Such arguments were essential in the Cold War era when right-wing politicians like Republican senators Richard Nixon and Joe McCarthy attacked reformers and activists such as Randolph or Martin Luther King, Jr., for being communist dupes. Randolph had to demonstrate that he was on the right side in the Cold War. For Randolph, the easiest way to do that was to maintain his allegiance to the American form of capitalism, albeit with some socialist modifications. For the NECNP, the most important aspect of the economy was state planning to guide free businessmen, free farmers, and free labor unions toward the collective good. The committee desired that a new political party—a Party of the American Dream, they called it—would recapture the American reform spirit and help build greater economic security, political democracy, and social equality.

The Provisional Declaration of Principles made quite an impact on American politics. The next two issues of the *Antioch Review* carried over a dozen responses from leading politicians, intellectuals, and unionists including socialist Norman Thomas, Marxist writer Granville Hicks, philosopher Sidney Hook, and historian Arthur M. Schlesinger, Jr., who was about to publish his own forward-looking and progressive but much less radical political manifesto, *The Vital Center*. Unsurprisingly, the strongest words of praise came from Norman Thomas, the head of the Socialist Party. Not all of the reviews were positive. Franklin D. Roosevelt's former vice president Henry Wallace, who had just started gathering his own new Progressive Party with significant backing from American communists, was not supportive and in a curt reply to the NECNP's article said merely that he hoped the journal would provide him the space to deal with the future of American politics.

No one knows for sure if President Harry S. Truman read the Declaration of Principles, but he certainly felt the political pressure that had created it, as his own party began splitting apart over the very issues that the NECNP raised. Progressives such as Henry Wallace and more radical party members such as Randolph appeared to be spinning off, leaving the Democratic Party to the conservatives. President Truman refused to let the party return to pre-New Deal ideology and sought to keep his party together by adopting many of the NECNP's proposals. From late 1946 through the 1948 presidential election, Truman revitalized the Democratic Party platform, putting many of Randolph's issues, such as fair employment and the desegregation of the military, at the very center of national politics.

What made Truman decide to take up the mantle of Franklin D. Roosevelt? What convinced him to try to become a champion of civil rights when he had not been one in the past? There are several answers to these questions. First, Randolph's and the NECNP's political pressure forced him to act. To keep his party intact, he needed to develop a response to this new thunder on the Left. Second, the Republican Party was actively trying to bring black voters back into its camp by promising to fight for racial equality. Third, Truman was moved by the horrific racial attacks in the immediate postwar period. Unlike Presidents Wilson, Harding, and Coolidge who ignored the murderous rampages across the nation in the aftermath of World War I, President Truman did not sit idle. In December 1946, after the blinding of Isaac Woodard and the killings of the black Georgian veterans and their wives, President Truman issued Executive Order 9808, which set up the President's Committee on Civil Rights (PCCR). Echoing its Cold War context, the committee's broad charge was "to strengthen and safeguard the rights of the American people" in order to secure "domestic tranquility, national security, the general welfare, and the continued existence of our free institutions."[3] Although there were dozens of existing investigations into American race relations, including the monumental 1944 study *American Dilemma* authored by the Swedish economist Gunnar Myrdal and his staff, PCCR conducted its own fact-finding probe. Released in October 1947, the committee's report, aptly titled *To Secure These Rights*, severely criticized segregation and discrimination in all facets of American life but particularly in employment and in the military. And, among its recommendations, the committee argued for an immediate end to "all discrimination and segregation based on race, color, creed or national origin in . . . all branches of the Armed Services."[4]

Although a few observers at the time and more afterward considered *To Secure These Rights* a historic, groundbreaking, and pace-setting document, Randolph and other civil rights leaders had been saying the same things for decades. The difference, of course, was that now this critique of American society and the remedies that civil rights proponents sought had the president's seal of approval. To ensure that the president transformed his words into actions, Randolph had to challenge Truman to create fair employment and desegregate the military. No mere report was going to placate Randolph. Rather, to him, it was yet another sign that the moment had come to pressure the president, the federal government, and American political parties as hard as he could.

The battle over desegregation and an end to racial discrimination in the military was an old one. Every major American war since the Revolution had produced a serious debate about the role of black soldiers and full citizenship rights. The essential question was: why would African Americans—or other second-class citizens—put their lives in jeopardy if they were not treated like any other soldier, like any other veteran, like any other citizen? This question had carried special weight during World War II when President Roosevelt declared that the United States was the "arsenal of democracy." Now, during the Cold War, when President Truman and other politicians were asking soldiers to put their lives on the line and defend the country against communist threats around the world, the military's racist policies were a constant reminder of how far the United States had to go to live up to its democratic rhetoric.

During World War II, Randolph had pressed President Roosevelt to integrate the armed forces but achieved little result. The president had refused Randolph's call for an executive order banning discrimination and segregation in the military. In any case, Randolph's wartime attention had focused on the fight for fair employment. After the war, however, he renewed his campaign against the military, believing that ending segregation in the military was the key to defeating all discrimination. Randolph saw his opportunity to strike when in March 1946 the U.S. Army released its Gillem Board Report. In May 1945, President Truman's new secretary of war, Robert P. Patterson, had called on General Alvan C. Gillem, Jr., to investigate the army's policy toward African Americans. The Gillem Board acknowledged that racial discrimination had been a problem in the past, but it offered no solutions and no plans to end racial segregation in combat units, in military housing, and on bases. African American leaders were outraged. Along with a new ally, Grant Reynolds, a former Republican congressman from Harlem, Randolph formed yet another new civil rights group, the Committee Against Jim Crow in Military Service and Training. Formed in 1947, the committee, which had the support of over two hundred black leaders, initially sought to pressure the Democratic National Committee and President Truman into supporting legislation to end the military's racist policies. Nothing came of this action, but Randolph's next action was dramatic.

In the spring of 1948, President Truman laid out the major ideals of what became known as the Fair Deal. Among the president's charges to Congress was to pass bills outlawing lynching, the poll tax, discrimination in employment, and discrimination and segregation in the military. Truman also called on Congress to pass the Universal Military Training Bill, which would require military training of all able-bodied men. Originally, the bill also included a section abolishing Jim Crow in the military, but at the urging of army officials, Congress had removed that language. Upon hearing the news that the federal government indeed planned, as Randolph put it, to herd eighteen-year-olds into a Jim Crow army led by racist generals, Randolph and Reynolds requested an immediate audience with President Truman.

On March 22, 1948, the leaders of the Committee Against Jim Crow in Military Service and Training—namely Randolph, Reynolds, the NAACP's Walter White and Charles H. Houston, the National Urban League's Lester Granger, and the matronly civil rights activist Mary McLeod Bethune—sat down with President Truman. It was Randolph's fourth trip to the White House, and he knew that bluntness with the president yielded results. He informed Truman frankly that he had made several cross-country trips and told him that the sentiment among African Americans was that they would not fight in a segregated military. Frowning, Truman lost his patience with Randolph. But Houston was able to calm both men, and this allowed Randolph to request that Truman issue an executive order banning discrimination and segregation in the military. Truman made no promises, thanked his guests for coming, and abruptly dismissed them.

From the White House, Randolph and Reynolds took their fight to the halls of Congress. A week after their meeting with the president, the duo went to Capitol Hill to testify about the Universal Military Service and Training Bill, which would authorize a peacetime draft. Randolph told the senators on the Armed Services Committee that if Congress enacted a draft he would personally aid black men seeking to resist it. Such a statement led to a testy—and subsequently famous—exchange between Randolph and Senator Wayne Morse, the moderate Republican from Oregon. After a lengthy debate about Randolph's position, Morse finally told Randolph to expect to be prosecuted for treason if he encouraged others to fight the draft. Randolph shot back that he was prepared for jail, and he movingly expressed his beliefs in nonviolent resistance.

Unable to counter Randolph's eloquence, Morse grumbled that it was not the time or place for them to debate the legal meaning of aiding and abetting the enemy.

Congress passed the Universal Military Service and Training Act, and Truman signed it into law in 1948. Randolph immediately made good on his threat by forming the League for Non-Violent Civil Disobedience Against Military Segregation. The membership of the league was virtually the same as that of the Committee Against Jim Crow in Military Service and Training,

A. Philip Randolph (right) and Grant Reynolds (left) testify before the Senate Armed Serves Committee, 1948, Library of Congress, Prints & Photographs Division, NYWT&S Collection, LC-USZ62-128074.

but there were some important additions. In particular, the new group attracted the thirty-eight-year-old Bayard Rustin.

Randolph always had collaborators: Chandler Owen in the 1910s and Milton Webster in the 1930s and 1940s. Rustin was, however, his most capable lieutenant. Born in 1910 in West Chester, Pennsylvania, Bayard had a normal childhood to a point. His neighborhood was rather affluent, and his family, which ran a successful catering business, rented an enormous house. Rustin excelled at school, often making the white kids jealous. He went to college at the City University of New York as Randolph had twenty years earlier. In Harlem, Rustin also joined the American Communist Party, which had a well-deserved reputation for supporting civil rights. In 1941, he split with the communists when the party's Central Committee ordered him to stop agitating for civil rights. Communist Party officials feared that criticizing the United States' record on race relations and pushing for reform might harm the war effort particularly because after Germany's invasion of the Soviet Union Stalin needed America's help. Rustin and the communists parted ways, and it was at this moment that Rustin first met A. Philip Randolph. He had carefully avoided Randolph for years out of an antipathy for socialism. But now Randolph's political faith seemed more reasonable than the communist one he had just disavowed. Although Randolph hated the communists, he looked past Rustin's ideological commitment and gave him a post within his wartime March on Washington Movement. Randolph also introduced Rustin to a wider group of activists, including A. J. Muste, the head of the pacifist and civil rights-focused Fellowship of Reconciliation (FOR).

Rustin's work with FOR and its civil rights offshoot, the Congress of Racial Equality (CORE), was cut short in 1943. A Quaker, Rustin had invoked his religious right to avoid military combat service, which by World War II was possible. However, Rustin also refused to accept any alternative service, such as hospital work, that would have benefited the American war effort. The unsympathetic federal government sent him to prison at Lewisburg Penitentiary for four years. In 1947, Rustin reconnected with CORE and the growing civil rights movement. Sensing that their moment for significant reform was near, activists pushed hard on many fronts. Rustin was a key player. In addition to the efforts to desegregate the military, he collaborated with CORE to integrate public facilities in the South. In 1947, he joined a CORE group that tested the U.S. Supreme Court's ruling in *Irene Morgan v. Commonwealth of Virginia* (1946), which had declared segregation on interstate buses unconstitutional. CORE's 1947 "Journey of Reconciliation" involved an interracial group of civil rights workers riding in buses through southern states. In April 1947, Rustin and fifteen other white and black activists boarded Trailways buses in various southern cities and refused to sit according to custom: whites in the front and blacks in the back. Rustin and the other freedom riders were arrested. They immediately called the National Association for the Advancement of Colored People. But its president, Roy Wilkins, denied their plea for legal assistance, and Rustin took his turn on the chain gang.

After his thirty-day sentence was over, Rustin continued to work for peace and civil rights. In 1948, he again sought out Randolph. Together they began counseling young black men not to sign up for military service. Some African American leaders were quite critical of Randolph. Unsurprisingly, his old critic, the *Pittsburgh Courier*, called him an extremist and doubted seriously anyone would follow him. The National Urban League's Lester Granger, who had very close relationships with Pentagon officials, feared that white supremacists would use Randolph's testimony as proof that African Americans were not loyal and could not be counted on in a crisis. This time, however, blacks listened to Randolph. A public opinion poll of

*Bayard Rustin, 1964, Library of Congress, Prints & Photographs Division, NYWT&S Collection, WCBS-TV, LC-USZ62-121753.*

young black men in the New York daily PM revealed that over 70 percent of all respondents favored a civil disobedience campaign against Jim Crow in the military.

Randolph's nonviolent movement against the military worked. Bowing to the league's pressure as well as a challenge by the Republican Party, which had made military desegregation one of its presidential campaign issues in 1948, Truman issued two civil rights executive orders in July 1948. The first, Executive Order 9980, created new fair employment guidelines for the federal government. The second, Executive Order 9981, directed the military to desegregate and stop discriminating against African American soldiers and officers. To enforce Executive Order 9981, Truman set up the President's Committee on Equality of Treatment and Opportunity in the Armed Services, otherwise known as the Fahy Committee. By the time of the Korean War in 1950, military leaders had made great strides toward creating equality. And by the early 1960s, the U.S. military was one of the most integrated institutions in American life.

Randolph's victory, however, came at a professional and personal price. His actions caused him to lose supporters in the civil rights movement. For example, when President Truman issued his order to desegregate the military, Randolph did what he thought was honorable and attempted to disband the League for Non-Violent Civil Disobedience Against Military Segregation. To Randolph, the reason for the nonviolent protest group's existence had now passed. But activists like Bayard Rustin believed much more work remained to be done. Rustin and his young colleagues pleaded with Randolph to keep the organization intact. Nonetheless, Randolph asked his aide Rustin to schedule a press conference in the afternoon of August 17, 1948, to announce the dissolution of the league. Rustin did as he was told, but he also set up a press conference in the morning to denounce Randolph as a sellout. Despite the betrayal, it may have been Randolph who had the last laugh. Without the elder leader's name on the letterhead, the league floundered without clout or any way to raise money.

The other price for full-time political activism hit Randolph's home life. Around 1948, his beloved wife Lucille began to develop the telltale signs of arthritis. At the moment of Randolph's triumph over the military brass and their white supremacist allies in Congress, Lucille fell and broke her hip. She was confined to a wheelchair for the rest of her life. The sixty-two-year-old Randolph seemed to be pulled in all directions at once. He was running several organizations, editing the *Black Worker*, negotiating with President Truman, trying to keep his lieutenants in line, and now caring for his wife who had become an invalid. There are conflicting reports about Randolph's efforts as Lucille's nurse. Most of his biographers state that he tenderly looked after her, reading to her, purchasing the best foods, medicines, and health care. When he was away, she had the best care money could buy. But this was the root of the problem. In her later years, Lucille complained that Randolph had not been there when she needed him. Indeed, during those years, he was engaged in many civil rights battles along several fronts. Lucille and Phil never stopped calling each other "Buddy." However, there is no denying that Randolph's ability to do everything he wanted all at once was waning. He was no longer the unstoppable political force he had been in the early 1940s. Perhaps nothing illustrates Randolph's declining influence more than his two other major—and failed—undertakings in the late 1940s and early 1950s: his efforts to create a permanent fair employment practice commission and his attempts to transform the American Federation of Labor into a force for civil rights reform.

The movement to create a permanent, federal fair employment practice commission had begun before the end of World War II. In 1943, on the heels of the March on Washington Movement's efforts to save the wartime Fair Employment Practice Committee (FEPC), Randolph had established the National Council for a Permanent FEPC. In 1945 and 1946, Randolph and the National Council for a Permanent FEPC pushed hard to get an FEPC bill passed. Unlike the creation of the wartime FEPC, success in Congress now depended on the political strength of Randolph's allies in the House and Senate, and not the pressure he could put on the president. And, as he quickly realized, the representatives and senators who purportedly backed the FEPC could not or would not deliver. New Jersey's liberal Democratic representative Mary T. Norton led the first attempt to enact a permanent FEPC law. Despite the fact that during the 1944 presidential election, the Republican Party had pledged its support for a new federal FEPC, Norton's Republican colleagues conspired with southern Democrats to bottle up the bill inside the House Rules Committee. Unable to counter the conservatives' chicanery, Norton failed to get her bill out of that committee. Thus the first push for a permanent FEPC ended, killed by the effective use of the bylaws of the House of Representatives.

In 1946, Randolph and his supporters could do no more than start the process again during the next session of Congress. This time, they focused on the Senate. Unfortunately for Randolph and the National Council for a Permanent FEPC, the results were perhaps even more discouraging. Senator Dennis Chavez, a Democrat from New Mexico, led the charge. His bill was essentially the same as Norton's. As with the House, the public hearings went smoothly. Only two people spoke out against the legislation. Somewhat surprisingly, the American Federation of Labor, the organization to which Randolph had belonged for more than a decade and which had supported the wartime AFL to some degree, sent its legislative representative to oppose the bill. The AFL's leaders thought the bill gave the federal government too much power over unions. Then, a citizen appeared before the Senate claiming that the FEPC bill was the first part of a communist-inspired plot to take over the federal government. Although still a socialist, Randolph went out of his way to convince the public and politicians of the notion that the FEPC bill was not part of a communist plot. Presaging the Cold War fights about fair employment, some critics had already tried to redbait the NCPFEPC.

Making matters worse for Randolph were people such as New York Congressman and procommunist radical Vito Marcantonio, who had proposed his own FEPC bill. In his public statements and before Congress, Randolph was careful to distance himself from the extreme left wing in American politics. Moreover, as would become his habit, he emphasized the prodemocracy aspects of fair employment. He told the congressmen that without a federal fair employment practice commission the country might drift toward Hitlerism, becoming a nation without any civil rights for racial and ethnic minorities. His rhetoric was successful, at least to a point. It was enough to sway the committee members and get the bill sent to the Senate floor.

On the floor, conservative senators staged a filibuster to defeat the bill. The idea was to keep the Senate in debate until the supporters of the FEPC gave up. But this was no ordinary filibuster. One might have expected Senator Chavez to fight tooth and nail for this landmark civil rights bill. In fact, he did not. To close observers, such as the *New York Times*' Pulitzer Prize-winning

The Girl Friends for FEPC Fight present a check of $500 to A. Philip Randolph. 1950, Library of Congress, Prints & Photographs Division, NYWT&S Collection, photograph by Rufus Merritt, LC-USZ62-104695.

reporter Arthur Krock, the fight over the FEPC bill was "phony." Krock called the filibuster a "banking-hours filibuster." After conservative Democrats and Republicans made their speeches against fair employment, they huddled with Chavez, smiling and laughing. Then, Chavez and Georgia's Democratic senator Richard Russell agreed to recess the Senate at 4:30 p.m. so that no one was inconvenienced and everyone could get home in time for dinner. According to Krock, the entire episode was "pure political theatre." It was, however, a theater in which Randolph could not perform. He was a frustrated member of the audience who could only sit and watch as Senator Chavez's halfhearted attempt to pass the FEPC law was defeated.[5]

In the wake of these legislative defeats, attention and hope fell back on President Harry S. Truman, whose initial position on fair employment was not positive. In fact, he had caused the ultimate demise of the wartime FEPC. But as the 1948 presidential election approached, Truman reevaluated his view on the creation of a permanent FEPC and took some advice from the President's Commission on Civil Rights. In February 1948, he delivered his famous civil rights address to a joint session of Congress in which he called on legislators to close the gap between American ideals and American practices. However, very little of Truman's civil rights agenda made it into law. Thus, on July 26, 1948, he used his presidential powers and issued Executive Order 9980. This was a far cry from the one that Randolph and Roosevelt had put together. Truman's order, which created a watchdog agency called the Fair Employment Board, dealt only with federal civil service employees and offered few avenues for redress or even protections from racial discrimination. Thus, despite Randolph's forceful efforts, his attempts at a state-centered solution to employment discrimination seemed hopelessly stalled in the nation's capital.

As with the postwar push for fair employment, Randolph's bid to transform the labor movement, particularly the AFL-CIO (which had reunited in 1955 in order to strengthen the labor movement), seemingly went nowhere. In his radical Harlem days, he had been harshly critical of the AFL. Once Randolph joined the federation in 1934, he lobbied to change the organization from the inside. At the 1934 annual AFL convention, Randolph took the floor, criticized the labor organization for tolerating racial discrimination, and called on his union brothers to take effective action. Specifically, he proposed that the AFL leadership make an in-depth inquiry into the racial practices of member unions and report the findings at the next convention. The committee tasked to do the investigation actually did its homework and presented damning conclusions to the AFL's Executive Council well before the 1935 convention. Unable or unwilling to deal with the truth, the Executive

Council substituted that report on racial discrimination with its own and presented the whitewashed version to the delegates at the 1935 meeting. Randolph was aghast, but that convention had other issues to deal with. It was at this convention that John L. Lewis and his followers broke from the AFL, later forming the Congress of Industrial Organizations (CIO) in 1937. Marching out of the conference room, Lewis encouraged Randolph to join him. In fact, Lewis's union, the United Mine Workers, was one of the few AFL unions that had engaged in integrated organizing. Wishing his friend well, Randolph and the BSCP decided to stay within the AFL. He told Lewis that he had no quarrel with the splinter unions, but he felt obliged to stay with the AFL and carry on the fight against racial discrimination. Randolph carried on the lonely fight with only Milton Webster to offer moral and tactical support. At the 1936 AFL convention in New Orleans, Randolph rose again to attack employment discrimination, charging that segregated locals and unfair practices were in fact spreading what he called trade union fascism. When Randolph had finished, Charles MacGowan of the Boilermakers took the floor to denounce Randolph. Afraid of no one, Randolph retorted that he did not care what anyone thought of his ideas or whom he offended. He was going to continue to fight until the AFL changed its policies and practices.

For over twenty-five years, Randolph carried on, despite the threats and tantrums of his fellow unionists. He continued long after the AFL seemed to care. Frequently when he took the podium, convention attendees either walked out for a smoke or drink or stayed and heckled him. Randolph never let them get his goat, as his generation would have put it. As the *New York Times*' labor reporter A. H. Raskin commented, Randolph always took the punishment with his usual dignity. That said, over time, Randolph developed a clear strategy and rhetoric to eliminate discrimination within the AFL. His strategy reached a climax during the middle of the Cold War at the 1959 AFL convention.

Randolph's plan was to have the AFL approve a convention resolution that would expel those unions that discriminated against African Americans. In one sense, Randolph was not asking for a dramatic change of AFL policy and practice. The organization's leaders had thrown out unions before: in 1937 the federation had expelled the CIO unions, and in the 1950s it had kicked out the Teamsters and Longshoremen for being corrupt. For Randolph the ultimate corruption was not graft but racial injustice. With his Resolution No. 32, he asked the AFL to expel the Brotherhood of Locomotive Firemen and Enginemen and the Brotherhood of Railroad Trainmen, because they had barred blacks from membership and thus violated the AFL-CIO

Constitution, which pledged "to encourage all workers without regard to race, creed, color, national origin or ancestry to share equally in the full benefits of union organization."[6] In support of his motion, Randolph laid out the case against the locomotive and railroad workers and argued stridently along democratic lines. Both unions had a long, notorious history of racist behaviors and conspiracies. "What kind of trade union democracy is that?" Placing his argument in the Cold War context, he reminded the AFL, "How can you go to the workers of Africa and Asia and talk about trade union democracy with unions affiliated with the AFL-CIO with a color bar in their constitutions? . . . It just can't be done."[7]

During the Cold War era when Americans took pride in being the most democratic people on the planet, Randolph's forceful words struck a nerve. Indeed, how could America spread democracy abroad to Africa and Asia when it was not democratic at home? This was the exact point that world leaders, especially those allied with the Soviet Union, were making. Randolph reiterated his argument on the final day of the convention when he introduced a blanket resolution to expel any union—not just the locomotive and railroad workers' unions—that practiced racial discrimination. Whereas in previous conventions the attendees either ignored or booed Randolph, this time, AFL-CIO President George M. Meany took it upon himself to answer Randolph.

To rebuff Randolph, Meany fell back to that cherished but not always observed AFL precept: the federation did not intend to interfere with the rituals, policies, and practices of its constituent unions. Moreover, he asserted that many of the unions that Randolph criticized actually had a good record on racial tolerance and civil rights. Thus, Meany indicated that Randolph's motion should be dismissed. In response, Randolph charged that no corrupt union should have a home in the AFL. At this Meany lost his cool and patience. He fired back that Randolph did not speak for everyone and accused him of wanting to destroy unions. "Who the hell appointed you as the guardian of the Negro members in America?" Meany blasted.[8] Taken off guard at the vehemence of Meany's attack, Randolph lost his fight to force the AFL-CIO to end its support of unions that discriminated against blacks. However, this was not the last time Meany and Randolph would clash over the issue.

Both Randolph and Meany spent the first few weeks after the raucous 1959 San Francisco convention mending fences. Meany told reporters that his cross words were nothing more than convention language and that he and Randolph remained friends and colleagues. Randolph accepted the apology and forgave Meany. The niceties did not last, and by the end of the year, the two labor leaders again feuding. In late 1959, Randolph assumed the presidency of a new labor group, the Negro American Labor Council (NALC), whose aims were to fight for civil rights in the AFL-CIO and secure rights of membership for all black workers within unions. The radical members of the NALC, like Richard Parish, were very critical of the AFL-CIO's Executive Council. Meany took this development as a slap in the face and a direct challenge to his leadership. Thus, he refused Randolph's request to attend the first NALC convention in 1960. Meany and Randolph's relationship continued to sour. When pressured about the council's demand that the AFL-CIO treat unions that discriminated against blacks the same way they treated those unions that were procommunist or corrupt, Meany stated that he did not see how racial discrimination and communist infiltration were similar. In 1961, Meany had had enough and sought to end the war of words by having Randolph, who since 1955 had been an AFL-CIO vice president, formally censured by the Executive Council. In essence, the AFL-CIO turned its back on Randolph. For the next year, Randolph worked to regain Meany's trust. Finally in 1962, he convinced the AFL-CIO president to appear before the NALC's annual meeting. But as Randolph healed one rift, another soon opened. The young black radicals within the council opposed the renewed friendship. The NALC's James Houghton called Randolph the greatest Uncle Tom in the American labor movement.

Houghton's verbal attack demonstrated to Randolph that he was no longer leading the vanguard for social and political reform. Randolph had lost some of his stature. By the early 1960s, he clearly had less influence among black workers than he had immediately following World War II. The early Cold War period had proven more difficult than he could have predicted. Randolph was very adept at putting his causes—whether the desegregation of the armed forces, fair employment, or the transformation of the AFL-CIO into a pro-civil rights labor organization—into the context of America's global conflict with communism. An integrated military, the establishment of equal employment opportunities, and the future of America's largest federation of unions were not merely personal issues for African-American workers. As Randolph, and even his opponents like George Meany, continually pointed out, these issues were of monumental and consequential importance in the battle to win the Cold War. Randolph's record in these specific battles is mixed. Although the military became one of the most integrated institutions in American society, fair employment and changing the labor movement were harder fights to win. Moreover, it seemed that the harder Randolph pushed, the more resistance he met from his opponents and his supporters. By the early 1960s, his own labor federation had censured him, and he had lost the personal ties he had made with labor unionists like Meany and younger radicals like James Houghton. When we consider the added pressure of taking care of an invalid spouse, it is easy to see how these years took their toll on Randolph. By 1962, Randolph was tired, having spent most of his political capital and personal energy. But like so many times before, he was down but not out. He had within him one more grand idea, the staging of an event that was to become an icon in American history: the 1963 March on Washington.

## Notes

1. Congress, Senate, Committee on Armed Services, *Universal Military Training: Hearings before the Committee on Armed Services*, 80th Cong., 2nd session, 30 March 1948, 689.

2. John Woolley and Gerhard Peters, eds. and compilers, "Political Party Platforms," in *The American Presidency Project* www.presidency.ucsb.edu/platforms.php (accessed 24 July 2005).

3. President's Committee on Civil Rights, *To Secure These Rights: The Report of the President's Committee on Civil Rights* (Washington, D.C.: GPO, 1947), viii.

4. President's Committee on Civil Rights, *To Secure These Rights*, 162.

5. Arthur Krock, "A Filibuster that Kept Bankers' Hours," *New York Times*, 14 February 1946: 23.

6. AFL-CIO, *Proceedings of the Third Constitutional Convention of the AFL-CIO*, vol. 1 (Washington, DC: AFL-CIO, 1960), 479.

7. AFL-CIO, *Proceedings of the Third Constitutional Convention of the AFL-CIO*, 483, 485

8. A. H. Raskin, "Meany, in a Fiery Debate, Denounces Negro Unionist," *New York Times*, 24 September 1959: 1.

CHAPTER FIVE

# The 1963 March on Washington: Randolph's Finest Hour

> Why is it necessary to have the march on Washington? Why is it that we have the civil rights revolution? The reason for existence of the civil rights revolution is that Negroes are not yet fully free.
>
> —A. Philip Randolph, 1963[1]

In early December 1962, A. Philip Randolph sat in his Brotherhood of Sleeping Car Porters office at 217 West 125th Street, Harlem. As usual, he was impeccably dressed, still wearing a suit, vest, and tie, and, as always, he had come with a newspaper in hand. The city's newspapers were carrying stories about daily occurrences in the renewed struggle for civil rights. These reports stirred mixed emotions in Randolph. On the one hand, he had waited his entire adult life to see a mass movement of people fighting to secure first-class citizenship rights for African Americans. On the other hand, he realized that he was no longer part of the movement's vanguard. Rather, at seventy-three he was its elder statesman, revered but not often consulted. New younger leaders like the Southern Christian Leadership Conference's Martin Luther King, Jr., and the NAACP's Roy Wilkins were capturing the eye of the media, and were inspiring people to join them.

While pondering his role in the civil rights movement and thinking about his ability to contribute to it, Randolph's friend and collaborator Bayard Rustin walked into his office. Randolph and Rustin had long since patched up their differences. In fact, Randolph never mentioned what had happened in 1948. Holding grudges was not in his character. There were more important things to talk about, like how to further propel the civil rights movement.

Randolph and Rustin chatted about the state of the movement and what they could do to broaden support for it. After a short discussion, both fell back on an idea that Randolph had discussed the previous year. At the 1961 meeting of the Negro American Labor Council (NALC), Randolph had first proposed a new march on Washington, D.C., to protest the atrocious record that the federal government had amassed relating to educational and employment opportunities for black Americans. In 1961, there were more—rather than fewer—black students in segregated public schools in the United States than had been the case in 1954, the year of the U.S. Supreme Court's *Brown v. Board of Education* decision. The job picture for African Americans was also disconcerting, to say the least. After gaining ground in the mid-1940s and early 1950s, blacks' incomes had slipped in comparison to those of whites. The average black worker now earned about half of the salary of the average white worker. Moreover, unemployment rates among African Americans in the labor force were skyrocketing. In 1960, the national unemployment rate among blacks was 10 percent, twice that of whites. In some cities, the conditions were worse. In Milwaukee, Wisconsin, for instance, there were almost three times as many unemployed African Americans (11 percent) as unemployed whites (4 percent). In his 1961 NALC convention speech, Randolph noted that the high unemployment levels were sowing the seeds of discontent. To Randolph and Rustin, the only path to restoring hope was to demonstrate publicly in order to show that a large cross-section of Americans, white and black, rich and working class, supported civil rights. Thus, on that December day, these two civil rights leaders dedicated themselves to organizing a march of the masses on Washington. They wanted to make the protest they had threatened in 1941 become a reality in 1963. Randolph's job was to supply the ideas and gather the political support; Rustin's job was to handle all the logistics.

By the mid-1950s, Rustin was no longer a foot soldier in the civil rights revolution, but a leader with exceptional skills at planning events and demonstrations. However, to some, Rustin was also a liability, a man with personal baggage whose actions affected the reputations of the organizations with which he was connected. In January 1953, Rustin was arrested in Pasadena, California, on a "morals charge." Local police had found Rustin in a parked car engaged in sex with two men. They were quickly tried and convicted for homosexual activity and sentenced to thirty days in jail. At the time, Rustin worked for the nonviolent civil rights group, Fellowship of Reconciliation (FOR). FOR's A. J. Muste felt he had no other choice than to dismiss Rustin. Indomitable, Rustin continued to work without any affiliation. In 1955, when the bus boycott started in Montgomery, Alabama, Rustin rushed there to see if he could help. At first, the leaders of the Montgomery Improvement Association (MIA)—the Reverend Martin Luther King, Jr., the Reverend Ralph Abernathy, and E. D. Nixon, the president of the local chapter of the Brotherhood of Sleeping Car Porters and the NAACP—viewed him with suspicion. After all, he was an unemployed ex-con, an ex-communist, and a homosexual. These indelible marks on his identity would no doubt become public, and they might have tainted the Montgomery Improvement Association and led to the defeat of the boycott. But Rustin had two things going for him. He was an exceptional organizer, and he had Randolph's blessing. That was good enough for E. D. Nixon. Rustin stayed with the MIA long enough to help organize the boycott and infuse the movement with his typical optimism. In 1957, following the boycott, he helped King establish the Southern Christian Leadership Conference, the organizational arm of King's civil rights campaign. Quickly, the SCLC made its presence felt as it undertook a broad campaign to radically transform American race relations.

With considerable interest, both Rustin and Randolph had watched SCLC as well as other new developments in the civil rights movement. They saw how King and others were altering the political landscape. They were quite aware that the late 1950s constituted a watershed period for the struggle for racial equality, equity, and justice. The sudden and dramatic changes were hard to explain fully. But by 1960—after the U.S. Supreme Court's *Brown* decision, after the controversy surrounding the integration of Little Rock's public high school, after the murder of the young black Chicagoan Emmett Till, and after the well-publicized acts of civil disobedience like the student sit-ins—the civil rights movement was finding more and more fertile ground in America. And it was clear to both Randolph and Rustin that the time had come for decisive action to make dramatic improvements in the lives of African Americans.

Thus in December 1962, motivated by their deep, abiding passion to improve the lives of all Americans, especially black Americans, Randolph and Rustin decided to work together on the march on Washington. The goal of the march was to help usher in a new age of justice and advance long-stalled civil rights legislation. But there was more to it than that. For Randolph, collaborating with Rustin was a necessity. Welcoming him back was not merely a reflection of Randolph's princely, magnanimous nature. At seventy-three, he could no longer act alone. He had to have help. Once athletic and powerful, his body was starting to give out. During the 1950s, Randolph had fainted several times while on the lecture circuit. At age fifty-two, Rustin still had unbounded energy. For his part, Rustin needed Randolph. The main civil rights leaders of the day, especially the NAACP's Roy Wilkins, cast a skeptical eye toward Rustin. But Randolph did not seem to care about Rustin's past, perhaps because he knew all about being the outsider and the misfit. Moreover, Randolph knew that they could carry out a march. It was a matter of preparation and planning. And, Randolph and Rustin were abundantly confident. In fact, it was not even their first march on the capital.

Before the famous 1963 March on Washington, Randolph had been involved in several other demonstrations. In the spring of 1956, Randolph had called on African American civil rights leaders to gather for a closed-door conference in Washington, D.C., to discuss the situation for African Americans and the Southern Manifesto, a statement signed by more than one hundred southern legislators signaling their refusal to desegregate. It did not take long for civil rights leaders to identify one of their main obstacles: President Dwight D. Eisenhower. Ike was neither a racist like Mississippi's Democratic senator James Eastland, an outspoken opponent of civil rights, nor was he a stalwart supporter of civil rights reform. After the 1954 *Brown* decision, Eisenhower pursued enforcement of integration slowly, carefully avoiding conflict with southern whites who were increasingly voting for Republicans. The 1957 meeting of civil rights leaders, namely Randolph, Rustin, Martin Luther King, Jr., and the new head of the NAACP, Roy Wilkins, proposed a march on Washington to draw the nation's attention to the deteriorating conditions for blacks in the South. Capturing the new feeling of the era in which religion seemed more important than socialist or labor politics, Randolph coined his march the "Prayer Pilgrimage for Freedom." To support his rally, he secured the backing of Martin Luther King, Jr., and Roy Wilkins. The three-hour event, which was the first black mass protest march in Washington, took place on May 17, 1957, the third anniversary of the U.S. Supreme Court's desegregation ruling. In what became the largest civil rights demonstration up to that date, over 25,000 marchers sauntered slowly to the Lincoln Memorial. At its steps, the crowd sang, prayed, and listened to speakers who praised the Great Emancipator and decried the indifference of Eisenhower. By all accounts, the pilgrimage had been a smashing success. Even W. E. B. Du Bois found something good to say about it to reporters, although he refused to mention Randolph by name.

Building on this momentum, Randolph helped to stage two more marches, one in 1958 and the other in 1959, to rally activists and to decry the continued slow pace of desegregation in the South. His "Youth March for Integrated Schools" took place on October 25, 1958. Nearly 10,000 black

*Roy Wilkins, A. Philip Randolph, Rev. Thomas Kilgore, Jr., and Martin Luther King, Jr., at the May 17, 1957, Prayer Pilgrimage for Freedom in Washington, D.C., Library of Congress, Prints & Photographs Division, A. Philip Randolph Papers, LCUSZ62-125026.*

and white students from elementary schools, high schools, colleges, and universities across the South and East converged on Washington, D.C. Randolph also secured some celebrity backing. Black singer, film star, and activist Harry Belafonte attended, as did baseball legend Jackie Robinson, and Coretta Scott King, who took the spot of her more famous husband, who was still recovering from a stabbing by an insane black woman during a book signing in Harlem earlier that fall. The march culminated with a delegation of eleven black and white students walking to the White House and asking to see President Eisenhower, who refused to see them. As Ike's secretary told them, unless they had a previous appointment, no one would allow them in. Afterward, the disappointed Randolph complained to reporters about the undignified reception. He had hoped that Eisenhower would have expressed an interest in integration.

A second "Youth March for Integrated Schools" took place on April 18, 1959. Twice as many marchers descended on the Capitol and assembled in front of the Washington Monument, where they listened to speeches by Martin Luther King, Jr., and Roy Wilkins. Randolph had prearranged for a new delegation of students and march leaders to meet with President Eisenhower. As it turned out, Ike was on vacation, and the group met with Vice President Richard M. Nixon, who had more civil rights credentials than the president: Nixon had served on several small federal civil rights boards in the 1950s. The vice president told the delegation that Eisenhower would not rest until African Americans had equal opportunities in employment, education, and politics. Still, Eisenhower failed to act in the last two years of his presidency to stem the rising rate of unemployment among black workers and the growth of segregation in the United States. For many civil rights leaders, including Randolph, the late 1950s constituted a period of missed chances on the part of the federal government to improve racial conditions in America.

For Randolph, the federal government's inaction presented a quandary. Although the marches were highly successful events, they did not seem to generate much besides empty platitudes from government officials. Rustin handled the marches' logistics superbly, and the demonstrations were controlled, orderly, and peaceful. For example, in 1957 at the pilgrimage, Rustin had a twenty-two square block area cordoned off for the marchers and for services to support them. He enlisted the support of local churches, and directed the event from his headquarters at the Uline Arena, the city's historic coliseum. One thousand church ushers from Baltimore served as an informal police force, keeping the peace, watching out for trouble, and helping those who needed medical attention. Although the marchers handled their own transportation and lodging, Rustin made sure that on the day of the march there was a free breakfast, and that the demonstrators marched in an orderly procession, organized into state delegations. Rustin also kept a keen eye on the banners and placards. Out of fear of violence, there were no inflammatory remarks. To be on the safe side, march leaders carefully watched and guarded the children. Rustin also supplied the children with songbooks and comic books, which focused on the civil rights movement. Each march Rustin organized remained nonviolent and without any problems. For his part, Randolph had rallied civil rights leaders into a unified stance, at least publicly. In addition to getting high-profile celebrities to pound the pavement, he garnered the support of major labor unions. But what had the rallying and peaceful processions achieved? In 1957, in response to pressure from civil rights leaders, Congress had passed a civil rights law, but conservatives had gutted it before Eisenhower had signed it. And yet, Rustin noticed something that made another march seem like a good idea. Ten thousand people participated in the first march, and they got President Eisenhower's attention. Next Randolph and Rustin brought 20,000 marchers, and they got to see Vice President Nixon. What would happen, Rustin contemplated, when 200,000 blacks came to Washington? The president and Congress would have to take notice and act. To Randolph and Rustin, this new mass march was a foregone conclusion. The problem was deciding what to call it. After debating for a few weeks, Randolph insisted that it be the "March on Washington for Jobs and Freedom." The old socialist wanted to make certain that economic conditions got center stage attention.

Randolph immediately set out to get the organizational backing for his march. The initial reaction was not encouraging. King was angry. Of course, the SCLC's chief supported the march, but Randolph had not consulted with him first before announcing the march, and King was not pleased. The NAACP's Roy Wilkins was equally cool. He also agreed to help Randolph carry out the march, but wanted to know who the organizer was going to be. Wilkins, who assumed it was going to be Rustin, was not happy with Randolph's reliance on Rustin. After talking with Randolph, Wilkins called Rustin to chew him out and told him that he opposed his selection as chief organizer. On the defensive, Rustin wanted to know why. With his characteristic equanimity, Wilkins laid out his case against Rustin: He had been a draft dodger; he had been affiliated with communists and socialists; and he had been arrested on a sex charge. Quiet for a moment, Rustin thought about the connections between minorities, dissenters, and outcasts, all of whom suffered various forms of discrimination and prejudice. He suggested that the march's leaders ought to have courage and stand up for all victims of discrimination. While Randolph was prepared to do that, Wilkins responded that he was not, but would support the march anyway.

Having only Wilkins's tacit approval, Randolph next needed to call the major civil rights leaders together to discuss how to organize the march and how to raise funds for it. He had arranged for a meeting room in New York's Roosevelt Hotel for fifteen people, including various civil rights leaders and their lieutenants. But when Roy Wilkins arrived plans changed. Wilkins expected and wanted a "chiefs-only" meeting. He went around the table, fingering people to leave. Rustin of course got the boot along with Reverend Fred Shuttlesworth of the SCLC, James Forman of the recently formed Student Non-Violent Coordinating Committee (SNCC), Norman Hill of CORE, and Cleveland Robinson, a black unionist from New York City. Only six were left: Wilkins, Randolph, King, Whitney Young of the National Urban League, James Farmer of CORE, and John Lewis of SNCC. Once the unpleasantries were over, the Big Six, as they came to be known, got down to work. The group quickly decided that Randolph would be the march's leader. Wilkins tried without success to appoint a different organizer. Randolph refused to budge, arguing that the question before them was whether they planned to have a march or not. King, the former head of the Montgomery Improvement Association, supported Randolph's choice of Rustin. Conceding his position, Wilkins remarked that it would be Randolph's and King's fault if something went wrong. Finally, they set the date: August 28, 1963. All that was left now was the work: organizing the rally and lining up the politicians. The Big Six wanted to avoid the problems that the marches of the 1950s marches had encountered, namely a lack of presidential backing. The good news was that there was a new liberal president in the White House: John F. Kennedy, who believed that he owed black citizens a debt of gratitude since he thought that it was their votes that helped him win the White House by the narrowest of margins in 1960.

During the 1960 presidential campaign, Kennedy had made it clear that he was sympathetic to the civil rights movement. On October 16, 1960, candidate Kennedy had called Coretta Scott King to ask if there was anything he could do after her husband had been arrested while protesting in Atlanta. Coretta was appreciative and asked Kennedy to do whatever he could. Not yet president, there were limits to what he could do. But his brother and campaign manager, Robert, did pressure local authorities to release King. Eventually the cajoling produced results. The local judge dropped most of the charges but did convict King of a traffic violation and sentenced him to four months in prison. Owing to his legal team and the Kennedys' political pressure, however, King served only eight days.

In the spring of 1963, civil rights leaders came calling on President Kennedy to solicit his support for the "March on Washington for Jobs and Freedom." It was time for Kennedy to pay that debt incurred in 1960, although he was reluctant. The president struggled with civil rights, especially in 1962 and 1963. President Kennedy, his attorney general Robert J. Kennedy, and Vice President Lyndon B. Johnson worked hard to support the burgeoning civil rights movement while attempting to keep the Democratic Party intact. This meant that, when forced, the Kennedys took a strong stand, but left to their own resources they moved incrementally so as not to offend the conservatives in the party. For example, in 1961, CORE sent another group of freedom riders into the South to test the desegregation orders on interstate travel stemming from the 1946 Supreme Court ruling in *Morgan v. Commonwealth of Virginia*. Unlike the participants in the 1947 rides, the 1961 activists were brutally attacked, and this made the daily news. Biting his tongue and swallowing his disapproval of CORE's action, Attorney General Kennedy sent the FBI to investigate the attacks on the civil rights workers. He also sent six hundred marshals to quell the ensuing violence. Meanwhile, President Kennedy put into place his carefully crafted policy on antidiscrimination in employment. In March 1961, Kennedy signed Executive Order 10925, banning racial discrimination by federal contractors and creating the President's Committee on Equal Employment Opportunities (PCEEO), headed by Vice President Johnson, to enforce the order. Initially hailed by civil rights leaders and vilified by segregationists, Kennedy mollified his position by instituting "Plans for Progress." Under this program, a federal contractor avoided scrutiny and sanctions by the PCEEO if he signed a pledge promising to eliminate job discrimination within the company. Practically, Plans for Progress functioned as an employer escape clause and political safety valve. As a result, Kennedy made little progress on the jobs front, but his party held together, even though the seams were beginning to fray.

In 1963, political and social tensions seemed to reach a breaking point. That spring, King and the SCLC launched a major campaign in Birmingham, attacking segregation and employment discrimination. On May 3, the protests turned violent as the city's head of public safety Theophilus Eugene "Bull" Connor turned his riot police, attack dogs, and water cannons on peaceful marchers. Images of the violence in Birmingham had national and international ramifications. Like Truman before him, President Kennedy felt compelled to act to uphold America's special claim on democracy in the world. On June 11, 1961, in a televised speech President Kennedy outlined his new civil rights policy. Citing the violence in Birmingham as well as America's mission to spread democracy, Kennedy reminded Americans that the United States was committed to a worldwide struggle to promote civil rights and freedom. Explaining that black Americans did not enjoy the same rights, privileges, and prosperous conditions as white Americans, Kennedy offered a simple observation: Redress could come by street protests and violence or it could come as a result of landmark legislation. To that end, he told Americans that he would introduce a new civil rights bill, which would end discrimination in employment and segregation in public areas, integrate schools, and protect the right to vote.

Kennedy's bill was languishing in committee when news came that made the Kennedy brothers upset. A. Philip Randolph was planning another march on Washington. The president feared nothing good could come of it. There might be more Birmingham-type violence. Perhaps worse, the march might kill his civil rights bill, as congressmen and senators do not like to be pressured into reform. To see if he could do what Franklin D. Roosevelt did in 1941, President Kennedy invited Randolph and the other members of the Big Six to the White House. On June 22—a week after he had delivered his bill to Congress—President Kennedy and Vice President Johnson met with Randolph, James Farmer, John Lewis, Martin Luther King, Jr., Roy Wilkins, and Whitney

Young. Preeminent liberal and White House assistant Arthur M. Schlesinger, Jr., recorded the meeting. After welcoming his guests, the president explained his view of the situation in Congress. The civil rights bill was stalled, and in Kennedy's estimation it would be killed even with the most peaceful and somber march. The goal was success in Congress, and not a successful march. Randolph quietly countered the president's argument. Schlesinger thought it was Randolph's style to be quiet, but he had not been present in earlier meetings with Presidents Roosevelt and Truman. Age had indeed taken a toll. Moreover, Lucille, the love of his life, had passed away in the previous month, and Randolph was still visibly shaken. Nonetheless, he spoke with his usual haughty accent, but now less forcefully and more subdued. Still Randolph was very effective. Kennedy and Johnson tried to regain the upper hand at the meeting, but to no avail. As the civil rights leaders around the table took turns speaking, it was clear that they backed Randolph and were not going to budge. Finally King remarked that they could have both their march and the civil rights bill. Such optimistic thoughts carried the day. Finally Kennedy opined that they might all fail to achieve their goals but that it was more important to remain committed to working with one another. And with that, President Kennedy gave his consent to the March on Washington.

With President Kennedy's approval in hand and with a budget of only $100,000, the Big Six let Rustin work his magic. He and Randolph had initially planned on 100,000 marchers, ten times their first Prayer Pilgrimage. The setup, however, was roughly the same. Situated in a small, run-down office in Harlem, Rustin took care of every detail and prepared for any contingency. He sent thousands of letters and specially prepared pamphlets about the march to hundreds of churches, fraternal groups, labor unions, and business organizations. As was the case for his previous marches on Washington, individual participants were on their own to get to Washington, although Rustin offered logistical advice, suggesting that big groups charter buses and coordinate their arrivals so that everyone did not arrive and leave at the same time. The organizers provided basic amenities including food, loudspeakers, and security. There were plenty of first aid stations. As it turned out, however, there were not enough "comfort stations." This was not quite Rustin's fault. Twice the expected number of marchers came, and as a result there were long lines at the toilets all day. Rustin also took care of the publicity, distributing countless posters and selling tens of thousands of buttons. The latter were extraordinarily important as they generated income for the march.

By early August, everything seemed set, and then Randolph got some bad news. The American Federation of Labor-Congress of Industrial Organizations, the nation's largest and most influential labor organization, refused to support the March on Washington. On August 13, the AFL-CIO's Executive Council met to discuss the issue. It voted overwhelmingly to deny Randolph any endorsement, although the council did issue a statement in support of civil rights. United Auto Workers president Walter Reuther shamed his colleagues, calling their actions anemic. Perhaps unsurprised by his labor federation, Randolph quipped that his fellow councilmen produced a masterpiece of noncommittal noncommitment. AFL-CIO officials defended themselves saying that they did not want to upset the delicate balance in Congress where politicians were considering both civil rights and labor legislation. The AFL-CIO's lack of support was a serious blow. The backing of labor and civil rights organizations was essential to the Big Six. Previous marches on Washington had run deficits. In addition to selling merchandise, groups like the United Auto Workers had donated cash and supplies. Losing the AFL-CIO meant in practical terms that the march might further drain civil rights coffers. Additionally, this loss was the latest in a long list of snubs for Randolph. Ignoring, shouting at, cursing, and censuring Randolph was perhaps the last and greatest indignity that the AFL-CIO hoisted upon him. Federation president George Meany never lived this moment down.

Randolph arrived in Washington a few days before the march. On Randolph's first day in the capital, liberal Illinois senator Paul Douglas, who had been a supporter of fair employment legislation, hosted a dinner in his honor. The next day, the National Press Club offered a similar fete. Randolph gave a speech, a preview of the following day's sentiments. Demonstrations, he opined, were essential for a democracy and essential in the struggle for civil rights. Revealing his gradualist socialist philosophy he had guarded since the late 1940s, Randolph added that this civil rights revolution was not trying to overthrow a government. Rather it was a middle-class revolution intent on implementing our human rights and not on upending the American way of life.

August 28, 1963, turned out to be the perfect day for a march. The weather was divine. In the morning, temperatures hovered near sixty degrees, great for setting up the comfort stations, food areas, and the stage, and of course for marching. The afternoon temperatures stuck close to eighty, very comfortable for Washington, D.C., in August. Randolph was the grand marshal of the march, and the master of ceremonies. The march itself began a little late. Rustin and Randolph had made a logistical error at the very beginning of their planning. They estimated that 100,000 protestors would come. Instead, 200,000 showed up. The increased numbers were inspiring but strained supplies and amenities and stretched timelines. Around 11:30 a.m., the congregated marchers began their peaceful demonstration. The Big

*The 1963 March on Washington. Randolph is center, National Archives and Records Administration, RG 306: Records of the U.S. Information Agency, NWDNS-306-SSM-4C(36)6.*

Six, who were in front, led an integrated mass of people, the famous and the anonymous. Several hours passed before everyone was assembled at the Lincoln Memorial. Near 2 p.m., the formal program began. The world-renowned African American contralto Marian Anderson, who had given a famous protest concert at the Lincoln Memorial in 1939, was slated to sing the National Anthem to open the ceremonies, but she got tied up in Washington traffic, arriving too late and in tears. Camilla Williams, the soprano who was the first African American to sing with the New York City Opera, filled in. Randolph then gave his last major public speech, an oration that he had been waiting to give for more than twenty years.

"Fellow Americans," Randolph began, "we are gathered here in the largest demonstration in the history of this nation. . . . Let the nation and the world know the meaning of our numbers. . . . We are not a pressure group. . . . We are not a mob." Then savoring each syllable he said the words he had waited a lifetime to say: "We are the advance guard of a massive moral revolution for jobs and freedom." This revolution was not merely for the passage of civil rights legislation. The vanguard's goals were much larger. He told the crowd that like everyone else there he wanted fair employment, school desegregation, and integrated public accommodations. But, "we want a free demo-

*The leaders after the 1963 March on Washington. From left to right: Mathew Ahmann, executive director of the National Catholic Conference for Interracial Justice; Cleveland Robinson (seated); chairman of the Demonstration Committee; A. Philip Randolph (seated); Rabbi Joachim Prinz, president of the American Jewish Congress; Joseph Rauh, Jr. (bow tie), civil rights activist; John Lewis, Student Nonviolent Coordinating Committee; and Floyd McKissick, national chairman of the Congress of Racial Equality, National Archives and Records Administration, RG 306: Records of the U.S. Information Agency, NWDNS-306-SSM-4D(91)9.*

cratic society dedicated to the political, economic and social advancement of man along moral lines." Finally, Randolph made clear that the March on Washington was not the "climax" of the revolution. Rather, it was only the beginning of a new struggle "not only for the Negro but for all Americans who thirst for freedom and a better life." He reiterated that the marchers were the vanguard for this transformation. They were the "first wave" whose job was "to carry the civil rights revolution home . . . into every nook and cranny of the land . . . until total freedom is ours."[2]

After Randolph a veritable who's who in American life took the stage. There were speeches by Bayard Rustin, the UAW's Walter Reuther, the American Jewish Congress's Rabbi Joachim Prinz, the NAACP's Roy Wilkins, the National Urban League's Whitney Young, the SNCC's John Lewis, and of course the SCLC's Martin Luther King, Jr. There were also musical interludes provided by Marian Anderson, Bob Dylan, and Peter, Paul and Mary. Americans remember that the march was peaceful. In other words, there was no violence. The march did have its vocal critics such as George Lincoln Rockwell of the American Nazi Party and Malcolm X of the Black Muslims. There were even anti-March on Washington marches like the one that the anti-integrationist Indignant White Citizens Council staged in Austin, Texas. But even those were placid events. Furthermore, what Americans tend to remember about the March on Washington is neither Randolph's speech nor most of other orations or entertainment. Rather, Martin Luther King, Jr.'s, brilliant, stirring, and partially ad-libbed "I Have a Dream" speech constitutes our collective memory of the day. Additionally, many know of the controversy about John Lewis's original speech, which condemned the Kennedy administration's paltry civil rights record. In an eleventh-hour negotiation, Randolph got Lewis and his SNCC colleagues to modify their language. As the SNCC's Cortland Cox later told an interviewer, Randolph finally approached them and begged them to tone down the speech. "I waited my entire life for this opportunity," Randolph pleaded, "please don't ruin it."[3] Lewis and his fellow SNCC members obeyed their elder. After hours of lectures, songs, and prayers, the march ended, and 200,000 people went home. As the event closed down, Rustin found Randolph pensively standing alone. Rustin put his arm around him. He saw him crying, overtaken by the emotions of the day. Rustin paused and comforted him. Randolph then composed himself. He and the other march leaders walked to the White House for a meeting and public relations opportunity with President Kennedy. Soon after, Randolph too went home. On the way, he wondered about what he had said out loud at the Lincoln Memorial and about the meaning of the large number of protesters.

Despite the pledges of support from some liberal senators, notably Democrats Mike Mansfield of Montana and Hubert H. Humphrey of Minnesota, Kennedy's civil rights bill stalled in Congress. Randolph's March on Washington was more a moral victory than a political one. Only for a moment did the event seem to bring whites and blacks together to support civil rights. Only for a moment did Congress and the president seem fully behind the leaders of the civil rights movement. And only for a moment did civil rights

*President John F. Kennedy and administration officials meet with the leaders of the March on Washington Movement, August 28, 1963. A. Philip Randolph is center next to President Kennedy, National Archives and Records Administration, White House Photographs, John F. Kennedy Presidential Library, photograph by Cecil Stoughton, NLK-WHPST-STC277163-2TTT.*

leaders—with the exception of Malcolm X—seem unified. After the march, Americans returned to their old patterns. President Kennedy continued to battle Congress. Whites and blacks were no closer together, either literally or figuratively. And the coalition of leaders resumed their rivalry. The stalemated situation changed after a most unfortunate event. In the wake of President Kennedy's assassination, congressmen suspended their opposition to Kennedy's reform agenda. President Lyndon B. Johnson, the old "master of the Senate," bullied through Congress the 1964 Omnibus Civil Rights Act and after his reelection the 1965 Voting Rights Act. Although both laws were landmarks and represented a watershed in terms of the relationship between the federal government and civil rights, their immediate effects were limited. Meanwhile, the employment and educational conditions for black Americans and other minorities continued to worsen.

Increasingly, civil rights leaders were divided over solutions and tactics to improve the lives of America's poor, many of whom were African American. For some, the problems centered on the leaders themselves. For example, younger, more radical activists opposed King's and Randolph's penchant for short, highly visible demonstrations. Instead, many in the SNCC and CORE wanted sustained campaigns in which activists would stay until the work was done. The SNCC's Stokely Carmichael represented this kind of civil rights worker. During the 1963 March on Washington, the brash twenty-two-year-old remained in Mississippi on the committee's voter registration campaign. Younger leaders were also giving up on nonviolence, the cornerstone of Randolph's and King's philosophies. Perhaps the high-water mark of nonviolent civil rights activism came in March 1965 when King, Randolph, Rustin, and others led over 50,000 people in a peaceful march from Selma to Montgomery, Alabama. Five months later, on August 6, Congress passed and President Johnson signed the 1965 Voting Rights Act. However, just five days after that, a massive race riot broke out in a Los Angeles neighborhood. The Watts Riot, which resulted in $40 million in property damage, stemmed from an incident of alleged police brutality. Similar events sparked other riots in Cincinnati (1966), San Francisco (1966), Baltimore (1967), Chicago (1967), Milwaukee (1967), Newark (1967), and Cleveland (1968). The riots greatly disturbed Randolph, the old reforming socialist who never gave up hope that the national government would help to create equality and equity. He also opposed the ideology of the new African American radicals. "Black Power," the phrase that activist Stokely Carmichael made popular, encapsulated the loose constellation of ideas about black superiority, the need for self-help, the search to regain lost culture, and the pride in nationalist feelings among African Americans. Black Power adherents, such as the members of the Black Panthers, also rejected nonviolence in favor of self-defense. Randolph was unsurprised, but dismayed at these developments. For him, the emergence of radical black groups was inevitable because of the intransigence of whites and because in his reading of world history, revolution and violence seemed to come together. And yet, Randolph wanted no part of a movement that had any relationship with these black radicals. He believed that civil rights could only advance through some other ideology. To Randolph, the methodology was clear: social—if not socialist—reform. From 1963 until the end of the 1960s, he used two vehicles to drive his reform plans: the newly founded A. Philip Randolph Institute and the Democratic Party. The former developed and crystallized Randolph's ideas to fix the inner cities, which were not only erupting in violence but were also quickly becoming the epicenters of poverty in America. Randolph hoped that the latter would carry out his platform and put it into law.

In 1965, Randolph established the A. Philip Randolph Institute (APRI) to carry out the work begun at the 1963 March on Washington. The organization represented a broad coalition of groups including the AFL-CIO, CORE, and the NAACP. The APRI essentially replaced the Negro American Labor Council, which had become moribund by the early 1960s. Both organizations a similar goal, which was to promote labor and civil rights simultaneously. The institute was also a way for Randolph's legacy to carry on without him. By the mid-1960s, the seventy-five-year-old was becoming frail and sick. During the 1965 Selma-to-Montgomery march, Randolph looked and felt his age. Slightly emaciated and dehydrated, Randolph barely completed the demonstration. Rustin, who had gone with Randolph to Alabama, grew increasingly worried about his mentor and asked Randolph if he wanted to find a more comfortable place to listen to the speeches and sermons. Rustin remembered someone added, "Phil, please go get some shade. You might die here." Randolph tersely replied, "Can you think of a better place for me to die?"[4] In any event, the APRI was an attempt to ensure that Randolph's ideas and organizations would carry on, and it was a way for Randolph to create a job for Rustin: the vagabond activist had no steady organizational backing, let alone a steady source of income.

Randolph's second vehicle for reform was the Democratic Party. By the early 1960s, Randolph had come to believe the best chance for workers to get a new deal in society was to back Lyndon Johnson. In general, Randolph believed that Johnson's Great Society vision with its war on poverty provided blacks, and in fact all poor Americans, with opportunities for equal access to better public services, better education, and better jobs. But Randolph feared that none of these things were going to happen if Barry Goldwater, the arch conservative Republican candidate from Arizona, won the presidential election in 1964. Therefore, Randolph stumped for Johnson as he had never done before in a presidential election. Given that Randolph had denounced America's major political parties just fifteen years earlier, one could see Randolph's actions as a kind of hypocrisy. But in fact, Johnson's candidacy represented what Randolph, a lifelong socialist, always wanted, which was not a revolution but reform. Politically, Randolph was consistent, and he was loyal. He supported Johnson without any hint of criticism. That meant that Randolph, still a pacifist, publicly backed Johnson's military commitments in Vietnam. And it meant that Randolph publicly opposed any challenge to Johnson and the Democrats. At the 1964 Democratic Party convention in Atlantic City,

*President Lyndon B. Johnson awards A. Philip Randolph the Medal of Freedom, September 14, 1964, White House Photograph, Lyndon B. Johnson Presidential Library, photograph by Cecil Stoughton, C 710-12-64.*

Randolph tried to stop the Mississippi Freedom Democratic Party, the all-black challengers to the state's regular all-white Democratic convention delegates, from staging an embarrassing showdown. Randolph's radical colleagues in the civil rights struggle were angered at his election activities, which they saw as a betrayal. Johnson of course appreciated them, and before the election gave Randolph the Presidential Medal of Freedom, the highest honor the nation bestows on a civilian, and he gave Randolph a place at the reviewing stand during the inaugural parade.

Randolph's faith in President Johnson proved to be misplaced. Although sympathetic to America's disadvantaged, Johnson was also politically tied to the war in Vietnam. As a result, money flowed to the military and Johnson's domestic initiatives languished, and his administration seemed slow to address the serious problems of urban America. After the 1965 Watts Riot, for example, Johnson spoke out against violent protests, but offered no new plans to address the declining fortunes and opportunities for those living in ghettos. Rather, he called for a national summit, dubbed "To Fulfill These Rights," and tapped Randolph to preside over it. President Johnson's White House staffers were in complete control of the conference to ensure that there was no criticism of the president, who was suffering politically from the growing military quagmire in Vietnam. President Johnson's 1966 Conference on Civil Rights ended without fanfare or a significant plan of action. However, Randolph used the occasion to advance his own ideas about solving the inner-city crisis. He called for the creation and implementation of a Freedom Budget for All Americans, which proposed to invest $100 billion in urban renewal. Randolph's premise was that an economic investment of this magnitude would resolve the two primary problems in urban America: lack of jobs and a decrepit infrastructure. Although Randolph's Freedom Budget was original, it was based on historical precedent, such as the post-World War II Marshall Plan in Europe, notions of full employment, and earlier plans such as the National Urban League's Marshall Plan for American cities. What differentiated Randolph's Freedom Budget was the way he encapsulated these ideas.

Randolph's Freedom Budget made it to the halls of Congress but no further. By the time congressmen began to hold hearings on urban renewal, the federal budget started to collapse under the weight of the Great Society programs, the war in Vietnam, and other costly government commitments, such as the space program. The last two destroyed any chance for success in the war on poverty. When the federal budget began to burst in the mid-1960s, Congress chose to support Johnson's military efforts and slash his antipoverty initiatives. Cutting Great Society programs drew criticism from liberals, progressives, and radicals alike. It also spelled doom to the Freedom Budget, which was effectively shelved.

The Freedom Budget for All Americans was Randolph's last grand vision. By 1968, he was fast receding from public life. At nearly eighty, he was still feisty and committed to supporting labor unions and civil rights. But, aside from the APRI, he did not have much of a following, especially in black communities. The Brotherhood of Sleeping Car Porters, his original vanguard, was now in steep decline due to the transformation of America's transportation system. In April 1968, Randolph retired as BSCP president and six months later the union was dissolved and the porters merged with the Brotherhood of Railway and Airline Clerks. Further, the civil rights movement had developed along directions that Randolph did not support. Nothing demonstrated this more than the Ocean Hill-Brownsville controversy. In 1968, in New York City, parents, educators, politicians, activists, and students were embroiled in a conflict over local control of public schools. Some community leaders, particularly in predominantly black neighborhoods, wanted to govern the schools in their areas. In particular, these parents wanted to power to choose the teachers. In the Ocean Hill-Brownsville community, the school board, dominated by local control advocates, removed ten white teachers, many of whom were Jewish. The fired teachers immediately appealed to their union, the United Federation of Teachers (UFT). UFT leaders quickly organized protests, including several strikes, in order to defend the teachers' right to maintain their jobs, uphold union employment rules, and keep the union contract. Without hesitation, Randolph and the APRI weighed in on the thorny issue, coming down squarely in support of the teachers. This was the final straw—to some the final betrayal—and black radicals once again assailed Randolph for being a conservative Uncle Tom. Radicals also chastised him for being too close to New York City's Jewish community. The criticism directed at Randolph did little to affect the outcome of the controversy; in the end, the teachers won their case and were reinstated. Yet the controversy showed how far Randolph had traveled away from his flock. African Americans had refused to follow the self-proclaimed leader of the vanguard, and they completely misunderstood his intentions. Fundamentally, he remained a trade unionist at heart. Moreover, he opposed bigotry in any disguise whether it was white racism, black power, or anti-Semitism. To Randolph, prejudice only fueled the fires of selfish discontent and further delayed socialist reform.

The Ocean Hill-Brownsville episode took its toll on Randolph. Throughout 1968, he seemed to get weaker and weaker. In the spring, he visited the Mayo Clinic. He was home by summer, but then on a warm afternoon, Randolph left his Harlem office to return to his home in the still-grand but increasingly dilapidated Dunbar Apartments. Three young men followed him into the building and mugged him. Not finding enough money, they beat him up. Shortly thereafter, Bayard Rustin helped Randolph move to safer neighborhood. The next year, Rustin also organized a tribute celebration for Randolph's eightieth birthday at New York's opulent Waldorf Astoria Hotel. C. L. Dellums, Randolph's successor at the BSCP; Corretta Scott King; George Meany (who sat at Randolph's immediate right all evening); Roy Wilkins; and Tom Powell, head of the A. Philip Randolph Leaders of Tomorrow youth group, gave speeches. Randolph ended the party with words of his own. Addressing the crowd of several hundred, he told them of his deep appreciation for the gathering and reflected on his life's work. To Randolph, his contribution to the "liberation of the Negro in America" was the establishment of "an alliance between the Negro and the American trade union movement." "The labor movement," Randolph said, "has been the only haven for the dispossessed." He also acknowledged that his achievements were a group effort. The BSCP, the MOWM, and his other organizations all played significant roles in fostering the nonviolent "on-going struggle" for democracy and integration. They were his socialist vanguard for reform. With them, he said, "we were able to reach out and build a movement of the Negro masses struggling to realize, upon this American soil, the freedom and the justice which they had so long been denied." Randolph reiterated his rebuke of young black radicals who questioned the relevance and importance of nonviolence, integration, and democracy. He urged them and those present to rededicate themselves to "the cause of freedom . . . reject racial separatism." "And we must," Randolph concluded his final public remarks, "have faith that this society, divided by race and by class, and subject to profound social pressures, can one day become a nation of equals, and banish white racism and black racism and anti-Semitism to the limbo of oblivion from which they shall never emerge."[5] Although few people heard it, his speech was perhaps the best encapsulation of Randolph's philosophy for social change. Society could advance only through the actions of the labor movement and only with a spirit of unity and appreciation for all people no matter what their race, creed, or color. Randolph was not the radical of his youth, but there was a remarkable consistency in these thoughts. He had an undying faith in the idea that the future of the nation was tied to ending the poverty that rigid class and racial privileges bring.

A. Philip Randolph lived another ten years, but quietly, without any relatives and with just a few friends to keep him company. On May 16, 1979, at the age of ninety, he died. The closest person to him was Bayard Rustin, who was in Washington, D.C., at the time of Randolph's death giving testimony before Congress about the current and future situation in Africa. While Rustin was speaking, someone slipped him a note with the sad news. As the *Congressional Record* reported, Rustin "crumpled up, shaking and weeping at the realization that his colleague, mentor, and friend . . . was gone."[6] Out of respect for both Rustin and Randolph, the House Subcommittee on Africa adjourned for the day. Rustin buried his old friend and made all the public arrangements, including a small memorial. Rustin also provided Randolph's epitaph for the press. As he told the Associated Press reporter who wrote the obituary that was sent to the nation's newspapers, "No individual did more to help the poor, the dispossessed and the working class in the United States and

A. Philip Randolph and Coretta Scott King shake hands at Randolph's eightieth-birthday party. Next to Randolph are (from left to right): Bayard Rustin, George Meany (glasses), and Nelson Rockefeller, Robert F. Wagner Labor Archives, New York University, Sam Reiss Photographs Collection, photograph by Sam Reiss.

around the world than A. Philip Randolph. With the exception of W. E. B. Du Bois, he was probably the greatest civil rights leader of this century until Martin Luther King."[7] No one familiar with the civil rights and labor struggles in the twentieth century would disagree with Rustin's words. No matter how much we have failed to remember Randolph and his enormous contributions to the movements for justice in the United States, he left an indelible mark on American history.

## Notes

1. "The 'March'—What Negroes Expected . . . What They Want Next," *U.S. News and World Report* (9 September 1963): 82.

2. NAACP, *The March on Washington for Jobs and Freedom: Speeches by the Leaders* (New York: NAACP, 1963), 3–4.

3. *Eyes on the Prize: No Easy Walk*, VHS (Alexandria, VA: PBS Video, 1986).

4. Bayard Rustin told Roger Daniels this story, e-mail, Roger Daniels to Andrew E. Kersten, 2 August 2005, in author's possession.

5. A. Philip Randolph Institute, *A. Philip Randolph at 80: Tributes and Recollections* (New York: APRI, 1969), 28–29.

6. *Congressional Record* 125, pt. 10 (21 May 1979): 12002.

7. "A. Philip Randolph Is Dead: Pioneer in Rights and Labor," *New York Times*, 17 May 1979: A2–A3.

# Afterword

> I don't ever remember a single day of hopelessness. I knew from the history of the labor movement, especially of the black people, that it was an undertaking of great trial. That, live or die, I had to stick with it and we had to win.
>
> —A. Philip Randolph[1]

Toward the end of his life, A. Philip Randolph sat down with Wendell Wray, a historian from Columbia University. After a long conversation about Randolph's childhood, his Harlem Renaissance years, and his work as a civil rights and labor leader, Wray asked Randolph to reflect upon his life. "What would you have done a little differently?" "Where do you feel you had any places you'd have done it better?" Randolph paused and without contrition said, "Well, I think in any life and in any struggle, when one looks back, one could say that perhaps here and there an approach might have been different, the level of intelligence of the people might not have been ready for this kind of an effort, and that I should have been more interested in cultivating the established leaders in the race, and perhaps some people thought I shouldn't have started in the American Federation of Labor with an attack on the leaders of the A.F. of L." But Randolph had no regrets at all. "I told it like I saw it, and so I think in the long run it has helped me. I have an inner satisfaction of having done what I thought was right at the time which I thought was propitious."[2]

This was not egotism. Rather, it was a reflection of how consistent and certain Randolph's thoughts and actions had been over the decades. In the formative years of the Harlem Renaissance, he had discovered socialism and kept the faith for his entire life. A lifelong socialist, he believed strongly that poverty and racial discrimination caused nearly all of America's problems. Undeniably, African Americans faced special and additional complications, but that did not mean the solution to their struggles was any different from those of the working class generally. Randolph thought that the federal government—in concert with state and local governments—had an obligation to improve the lives of America's poor and minority citizens through innovative, assertive, and progressive reforms. And, he never wavered, even when the politicians whom he trusted did.

In addition to spending his life fighting for labor and civil rights reform, Randolph struggled to energize as many supporters as he could. His political faith encouraged him to foster a vanguard, a group of forerunners who added political weight to Randolph's ideas and were foot soldiers for various demonstrations and marches. Furthermore, it was the vanguard's job to convince others to back Randolph's plans for social change. For much of Randolph's life, the Brotherhood of Sleeping Car Porters functioned as an institutional vanguard. But as rail traffic disappeared in the 1960s, so did the BSCP. At the end of this life, it was the A. Philip Randolph Institute, "my movement" as Randolph called it, which tried to lead the vanguard to further advances.[3]

Before Randolph left the oral history interview, the Columbia historian asked a final question: "Do you think history will remember you as a trade union leader or a civil rights leader?" "I think as both," he replied. But after reflecting for a moment, he decided that he had achieved more as a labor leader. The civil rights movement was perhaps "more glamorous" but he admitted he had not been able to "contact as large an area of people" as he had as the BSCP's president.[4] And perhaps that is why so many Americans have now forgotten Randolph. As labor unions seem to have a smaller and smaller impact on our lives, their leaders, their struggles, and their legacies have become blurry recollections of our collective past. But the fight lives on. The poverty and discrimination that Randolph railed against never disappeared. Any future movement to improve the conditions of the working class in the United States most likely will look back for antecedents. Thus, placing A. Philip Randolph into the gallery of great American heroes is merely a matter of time.

## Notes

1. A. Philip Randolph, quoted in a speech by Shirley Chisholm before the House of Representatives, 21 May 1979, *Congressional Record* 125, pt. 10, 96th Cong., 1st sess.: 12000.

2. "Reminiscences of A. Philip Randolph," 22 August 1972, Columbia University Oral History Research Office, 281.

3. Randolph oral history, 282.

4. Randolph oral history, 283.

# Note on Sources

There is an abundance of primary and secondary sources that document the life of Asa Philip Randolph. The A. Philip Randolph Papers at the Library of Congress and the oral history of Randolph at the Columbia Oral History Center are essential primary materials. The Federal Bureau of Investigation has an enormous file on Randolph; it is readily available in the FBI reading room or by requesting the document through the Freedom of Information Act. The FBI file on Randolph and other black American leaders is also available on microfilm. Although researchers should use the FBI's information with caution, it still provides a very useful window into Randolph's movements, actions, and thoughts. Other important government sources include congressional hearings, the presidential papers of Franklin D. Roosevelt, Harry S. Truman, Dwight D. Eisenhower, John F. Kennedy, and Lyndon B. Johnson, and reports of civilian and military government agencies. Other useful sources are newspapers, both white and black, as well as Randolph's magazines: *The Messenger* and *The Black Worker*. *The Messenger Reader* (New York: Modern Library, 2000) edited by Sondra Kathryn Wilson is a useful collection of stories, poetry, and essays.

The records of many of Randolph's organizations are also crucial research tools. The Brotherhood of Sleeping Car Porters' Papers housed at the Library of Congress are available on microfilm. Unfortunately, the main source of manuscript material relating to the 1941 March on Washington burned in a fire decades ago. However, there are some useful materials at the Franklin D. Roosevelt Library in Hyde Park, New York. Moreover, the microfilmed

Records of the Committee on Fair Employment Practice, housed at the National Archives, contain information relating to Randolph and the creation of Executive Order 8802. On issues of desegregation in the military, one should consult the U.S. Army's, Navy's, and Air Force's records at the National Archives as well as the related papers at the Truman Presidential Library. Finally, the microfilmed papers of the National Association for the Advancement of Colored People are essential for any researcher studying the African American experience in the twentieth century.

There are also many secondary sources focusing on A. Philip Randolph. The primary biographies are by Jervis Anderson, *A. Philip Randolph: A Biographical Portrait* (New York: Harcourt, Brace, Jovanovich, 1973); Paula F. Pfeffer, *A. Philip Randolph: Pioneer of the Civil Rights Movement* (Baton Rouge: Louisiana State University Press, 1990); and Cynthia Taylor, *A. Philip Randolph: The Religious Journey of an African American Labor Leader* (New York: New York University Press, 2005). I owe debts of gratitude to all of these scholars. Eric Arnesen will soon publish a comprehensive biography of A. Philip Randolph that should become the definitive interpretation of Randolph's life for at least a generation. There are a few good documentaries about Randolph: *A. Philip Randolph: For Jobs and Freedom* (San Francisco: California Newsreel, 1995); *10,000 Black Men Named George* (Hollywood: Paramount, 2001); and *Miles of Smiles, Years of Struggle* (San Francisco: California Newsreel, 1983).

Historians have focused most of their attention on Randolph's early years, particularly on the BSCP. See William Harris, *Keeping the Faith: A. Philip Randolph, Milton P. Webster, and the Brotherhood of Sleeping Car Porters, 1925–1937* (Urbana: University of Illinois Press, 1977); Joseph F. Wilson, *Tearing Down the Color Bar: A Documentary History and Analysis of the Brotherhood of Sleeping Car Porters* (New York: Columbia University Press, 1989); Jack Santino, *Miles of Smiles, Years of Struggle: Stories of Black Pullman Porters* (Urbana: University of Illinois Press, 1991); Melina Chateauvert, *Marching Together: Women of the Brotherhood of Sleeping Car Porters* (Urbana: University of Illinois Press, 1997); Beth Tompkins Bates, *Pullman Porters and the Rise of Protest Politics in Black America, 1925–1945* (Chapel Hill: University of North Carolina Press, 2001); and Larry Tye, *Rising from the Rails: Pullman Porters and the Making of the Black Middle Class* (New York: Henry Holt and Company, 2004). Eric Arnesen's *Brotherhoods of Color: Black Railroad Workers and the Struggle for Equality* (Cambridge, MA: Harvard University Press, 2001) is a broader survey of black railroad workers.

The 1941 March on Washington Movement has received limited scholarly attention. The best book remains Herbert Garfinkel, *When Negroes*

March: The March on Washington and the Organizational Politics for FEPC (Glencoe, IL: Free Press, 1959). Other useful works include: Lucy Barber, Marching on Washington: The Forging of an American Political Tradition (Berkeley: University of California Press, 2004); Andrew E. Kersten, Race, Jobs, and the War: The FEPC in the Midwest, 1941–46 (Urbana: University of Illinois Press, 2000); Merl E. Reed, Seedtime for the Modern Civil Rights Movement: The President's Committee on Fair Employment Practice, 1941–1946 (Baton Rouge: Louisiana State University Press, 1991); and Robert A. Hill, comp., The FBI's RACON: Racial Conditions in the United States During World War II (Boston: Northeastern University Press, 1995). Although dated, Richard M. Dalfiume, "The 'Forgotten Years' of the Negro Revolution," Journal of American History 60 (June 1968): 90–106 is still essential reading. Finally, John H. Bracey, Jr., and August Meier, "Allies or Adversaries?: The NAACP, A. Philip Randolph, and the 1941 March on Washington," The Georgia Historical Quarterly 75 (Spring 1991): 1–17 provides important insights.

The historiography of the civil rights movement during the Cold War is growing quickly. Standards include: Richard M. Dalfiume, Desegregation of the Armed Forces: Fighting on Two Fronts: 1939–1953 (Columbia, MO: University of Missouri Press, 1969); Donald R. McCoy and Richard T. Ruetten, Quest and Response: Minority Rights and the Truman Administration (Lawrence: University Press of Kansas, 1973); Carl M. Brauer, John F. Kennedy and the Second Reconstruction (New York: Columbia University Press, 1977); Taylor Branch, Parting the Waters: America in the King Years, 1954–1963 (New York: Touchstone, 1988); Taylor Branch, Pillar of Fire: America in the King Years, 1963–1965 (New York: Simon and Schuster, 1998); Taylor Branch, At Canaan's Edge: America in the King Years, 1965–1968 (New York: Simon and Schuster, 2006); Hugh Davis Graham, The Civil Rights Era: Origins and Development of National Policy, 1960–1972 (New York: Oxford University Press, 1990); and Jervis Anderson, Bayard Rustin: Troubles I've Seen: A Biography (New York: HarperCollins, 1997). More recent influential works are: Mary L. Dudziak, Cold War Civil Rights: Race and the Image of American Democracy (Princeton, NJ: Princeton University Press, 2000); Bruce Nelson, Divided We Stand: American Workers and the Struggle for Black Equality (Princeton, NJ: Princeton University Press, 2001); and Thomas Borstelmann, The Cold War and the Color Line: American Race Relations in the Global Arena (Cambridge, MA: Harvard University Press, 2001). Finally, the most authoritative account of the Ocean Hill-Brownsville controversy is Jerald E. Podair, The Strike that Changed New York: The Ocean Hill-Brownsville Crisis (New Haven, CT: Yale University Press, 2003).

# Note on Sources

This biography of A. Philip Randolph fundamentally deals with the nexus between the civil rights and labor movements. There is a vast historiographical tradition on this topic, including Sterling D. Spero and Abram L. Harris, *The Black Worker: The Negro and the Labor Movement* (New York: Columbia University Press, 1931); Herbert R. Northrup, *Organized Labor and the Negro* (New York: Harper & Brothers, 1944); and Robert C. Weaver, *Negro Labor, A National Problem* (New York: Harcourt, Brace, and Company, 1946). Recent books include Herbert Hill, *Black Labor and the American Legal System: Race, Work, and the Law* (Madison: University of Wisconsin Press, 1985); Joe W. Trotter, Jr., *Coal, Class, and Color: Blacks in Southern West Virginia, 1915–1932* (Urbana: University of Illinois Press, 1990); Eric Arnesen, *Waterfront Workers of New Orleans: Race, Class, and Politics, 1863–1923* (Urbana: University of Illinois Press, 1991); Michael Honey, *Southern Labor and Black Civil Rights: Organizing Memphis Workers* (Urbana: University of Illinois Press, 1993); Rich Halpern, *Down on the Killing Floor: Black and White Workers in Chicago's Packinghouses, 1904–1954* (Urbana: University of Illinois Press, 1997); Alan Draper, *Conflict of Interest: Organized Labor and the Civil Rights Movement in the South, 1954–1968* (Ithaca, NY: Cornell University Press, 1998); Daniel Letwin, *The Challenge of Interracial Unionism: Alabama Coal Miners, 1878–1921* (Chapel Hill: University of North Carolina Press, 1998); Eric Arnesen, *Brotherhoods of Color: Black Railroad Workers and the Struggle for Equality* (Cambridge, MA: Harvard University Press, 2001); Brian Kelly, *Race, Class, and Power in the Alabama Coalfields* (Chapel Hill: University of North Carolina Press, 2001); Bruce Nelson, *Divided We Stand: American Workers and the Struggle for Black Equality* (Princeton, NJ: Princeton University Press, 2001); Michael R. Botson, *Labor, Civil Rights, and the Hughes Tool Company* (College Station: Texas A&M University Press, 2005); and Paul D. Moreno, *Black Americans and Organized Labor: A New History* (Baton Rouge: Louisiana State University Press, 2006).

# Bibliography of Primary Sources

## 1. From Preacher Son to Socialist Radical

**a. Father's Advice: Reverend James Randolph to Asa Philip Randolph**
Extract from: "Reminiscences of Asa Philip Randolph," 11 July 1972, on pp. 79–81 in the Columbia University Oral History Research Office Collection. Used with permission of the Columbia University Oral History Research Center.

In this oral history, Randolph discussed the advice that his father gave him. Throughout his life, Randolph had a strong ethical sense and a passionate belief in his own abilities to improve the conditions for African Americans. James Randolph encouraged both his sons to help those who were less fortunate than they were.

> He said [to me]: "You have the ability to speak. Your brother has the ability to speak. You have books here that I've bought for you to read, in addition to your school work, and your school leaders and teacher, they love you and have faith in you, they believe you're unusually gifted chaps." He said, "You've got to make use of that, and this is what I'm trying to do for you, in order that you will not only be trying to make a dollar for yourself or become rich, but will create conditions that will help the people farther down who don't have your opportunities or don't have your gifts." He said, "This is the thing that we as a group must do, and you're not going to live merely by getting something here and there from people clandestinely. You've got to do things yourselves that will help other people as well as yourself."

He said, "This is why we stand apart in this community, but at the same time there is no Negro in this area who is too low for me to get out of my bed and go to help, if he is being assaulted by white racists. I may not know him, but if he's permitted to be subjugated and brutalized by white people and no Negroes help him, you are providing the basis for yourself being the objects of attacks and persecution by white people. Consequently the problem of one Negro is the problem of all of us. And whereas I don't think you should be going around to these pool rooms, liquor stores and things of that sort, in the last analysis, that you don't have the time to do and you shouldn't do. But the problem of one Negro is the problem of all Negroes, because there isn't a single Negro in Jacksonville who has any immunity from persecution by whites, and the persecution never comes by one white man, but it comes by mobs, and therein lies the major problem of our life."

He said, "When I say that I mean too that you have no right to hate anybody because of his color. You don't have the right to hate a white man because of his color. There are white men and women who have as deep a sense of Christianity as I have and your mother has or any Negro. Therefore they must be given support when issues arise that have social significance, meaning that the work that they do is of benefit to all Negroes."

He said, "We too must take that same position. We don't hate a boy who's white merely because he's white. But if someone tried to deprive you of your rights, you've got to resist it. You've got to resent it. You've got to fight against it. In the long run, it will tell. And I look forward to the time when your name will be nationally known around the country for the work you're doing not only for black people but for humanity."

## b. Randolph's view of American political history

Extract from: A. Philip Randolph, "The Negro in Politics" *Messenger* 3 (July 1919): 16–17, 20–21. Reprinted with permission from the A. Philip Randolph Institute.

In this article, Randolph summarized the political history of African Americans. He stressed the opportunities offered by the Socialist Party as a means for all working people, black and white, to influence politics.

> The Negro has had a pathetic and unpromising history in American politics.
>
> His eventful and hapless career began under the shadows of the institution of slavery, from which he had just emerged. He was played upon by two forces, viz., the open opposition from his former masters, on the one hand, and the fraud and deception of the white carpet-baggers, who swarmed South, like vultures, to prey upon his ignorance and credulity.
>
> We have but to take a glimpse into the history of the Reconstruction period, to witness his tragical fight, wrought by a paradoxical combination of his Northern Republican friends and his Southern Democratic enemies.

During this period the Negro was a political football between his former slave master and Northern political adventurers. The economic basis of this contest was the power to tax: to float bonds; to award franchise: in short, to gain control over the financial resources of the newly organized States. These were big stakes for which to contend. Hence, the carpetbagger used to enfranchised Negro to assist them in securing control over the Southern State governments and the Southern politicians fought the Negro viciously to prevent this Carpet-bagger-Negro political ascendancy.

This period of storm and stress gave birth to two significant social organizations, the Union of Loyal League of Negroes and the Ku Klux Klan, which attempted to protect the political interests of the Negroes and Southern whites, respectively.

They only served, however, to engender bitterness: to breed and to foster suspicion and hate between the races, which resulted in lawlessness crime and general social anarchy. These too, were natural, political and social consequences of the Reconstruction policy. The inordinate lust for power, overwhelming ambition to rule, the instinct to secure an advantage, impels individuals and social groups to adopt the policy of force, the policy of fraud, or the method of education: whichever policy is available, and is recognized as likely to secure the more permanent results.

Such were the political vicissitudes of the Negro in the South. The Ku Klux Klan and the tissue ballot were social and political inventions of intimidation to discourage the Negroes' participation in politics. The Thirteenth, Fourteenth and Fifteenth Amendments to the Federal Constitution, the Federal army and the Carpet-Baggers were designed to protect the Negroes' suffrage, in order that the Negro might entrench, reinforce and fortify the Republicans party's control over Congress. The lessons of this period had been hard, bitter and disappointing to the Negro. The army, the arm of protection of the Federal Government, had been withdrawn. The Negro office holders and their Republican supporters had been hurled from power. The Reconstruction legislation had been emasculated from the statute books. The Southern States had begun a systematic and organized campaign of nullification of the freedom and enfranchisement of the Negro. In fact, the Negro had been reduced to serfdom. And in 1876, the last vestige of Reconstruction governments had disappeared. And it cannot be maintained by the sober and dispassionate historian that the Negro had legislated and administered the State governments wisely and well. As he had ignorantly fought with and tilled the fields for his former master to maintain slavery, he had also voted to strengthen his Republican political masters, to dominate the government, only to be forsaken, neglected, naked to his enemies. No Negro, with a genius for leadership, had arisen in this period. So much for our Reconstruction history.

What has been the subsequent political course of the Negro?

The complete scheme of the Negroes' disfranchisement was in the process of development in the South. The South had resented and ignored the Fourteenth Amendment which had demanded a reduction in representation in Congress, if the Negroes' suffrage was restricted. Intermittent cries against this political brigandage were heard but finally subsided. The South continued to weave a fabric of law, the "Grandfather clauses," which gave legal sanction to an already general custom of Negro disfranchisement. The Republican Party, pretended friend and defender, had assented. Yet the Negro remained a Republican. Why? First, the Reconstruction legislation of the Republican Party had forged the "Solid South." The Solid South was dominated by the Democratic Party. The Democratic Party had striven to maintain slavery. It had been the father of the "Fugitive Slave Law," the nullification of the Missouri Compromise of 1820, and Chief Justice Taney had handed down the famous Dred Scott's decision, which gave constitutional sanction to the extension of slavery into new territory.

On the other hand, the Republican Party had been the party of the North, the refuge of the fugitive slave, the home of the abolitionists, Wendell Philips, Garrison, Lovejoy. And, Sumner was in power when freedom came. It had used the Negro as an office holder and continued to distribute political crumbs in the form of collectors of internal revenue, deputy collectors, registrars of the Treasury, Ministers to Hayti, Liberia and such places, that required no legislative ability, no intelligent understanding of the methods, objects and principles of government. In truth, the Negro office holders were mainly of the "rubber stamp" variety. But it was sufficient that the Republican Party had awarded jobs, to secure the indiscriminating and unquestioning devotion of the Negro. Thus, the Negro became as staunch a Republican as Irish a Democrat. It was considered race treason for a Negro to profess any other political faith.

Here and there an eccentric Negro had claimed to be a Democrat, but his claim was considered lightly. It is true that in New York City a tiny fraction of Negroes had bolted the Republican ranks and joined Tammany Hall, seeking political jobs.

There had also arisen among the Negroes a political schism, namely a belief in the virtue of dividing the vote. In support of this political heresy, it was maintained that by dividing the vote the Negro would be able to secure the good will of both parties: it was further maintained that it would create fear in the Republican Party which would result in its giving the Negro a fairer consideration, and that the Negro would be sure of political preferment, regardless of which party was in power. And in 1912 and in 1916 a few Negro leaders had professed sympathy for Woodrow Wilson as the Democratic presidential nominee.

The formation of the Progressive Party of 1912, had marked another important rift in the Negro Republican voters. The love for Roosevelt, the expectation of jobs and the general dissatisfaction with President Taft's attitude towards Negro job-holders in the South, had produced this alienation.

In the mayoralty election of New York City in 1917 occurred another change in the Negroes' political course. This change resulted in 25 per cent of the Negroes voting the Socialist ticket. This vote, too, it might be observed, was achieved despite the fact that heretofore there had been no Socialist vote among Negroes of New York State. . . .

I maintain that since the Socialist Party is supported financially by working men and working women, and since its platform is a demand for the abolition of this class struggle between the employer and the worker, by taking over and democratically managing the sources and machinery of wealth production and exchange, to be operated for social services and not for private profits; and further, since the Socialist party has always, both in the United States and Europe, opposed forms of race prejudice, that the Negro should no longer look upon voting the Republican ticket, as accepting the lesser of two evils, but that it is politically, economically, historically and socially logical and sound for him to reject both evils, the Republican and Democratic parties and select a positive good—Socialism.

The Negro, like any other class, should support that party which represents his chief interests. Who could imagine a brewer or saloon keeper supporting the Prohibition Party?

It is like an undertaker seeking the adoption of a law, if possible, to abolish death.

Such is not less ludicrous, however, than that of a Negro, living in virtual poverty, children without education, wife driven to the kitchen or wash-tub: continually dispossessed on account of high rents, eating poor food on account of high cost of food, working 10, 12 and 14 hours a days, and sometimes compelled to become sycophant and clownish for a favor, a "tip," supporting the party of Rockefeller, the party of his employer, whose chief interests are to overwork and underpay him. Let us abolish these contradictions and support our logical party—the Socialist Party.

### c. Randolph's Dispute with Marcus Garvey

Extract from: A. Philip Randolph, "Reply to Marcus Garvey," *Messenger* 6 (August 1922): 467–70. Reprinted with permission from the A. Philip Randolph Institute.

The public fight between A. Philip Randolph and Marcus Garvey is legendary. In this article, Randolph replied to Garvey's criticisms of Randolph. Randolph also chastised Garvey for his apparent ties to the Ku Klux Klan.

> Does Garvey employ the direct, honest and intelligent method of meeting the indictment of the editors of the *Messenger*? Dear readers, judge for yourself. Listen to this. Says he: "Before Owen and Randolph can speak of the failure of

any business and the incompetency of any individual to do business they should first prove their success and their competency to handle business." Think of such downright inanity and silly tommy-rot. In other words, a person must be a thief in order to have the right to criticize and apprehend a thief. A critic of acting or of the drama is not required necessarily to be an actor or a dramatist. A person may be the reviewer of books without being an author of books. A patient may know when his pain is relieved without being a doctor. Few economists are businessmen, yet they formulate the rules, laws and principles of business. Intelligent businessmen such as Morgan and Rockefeller employ economists to formulate, direct and guide their business policies. They don't rely upon the hit and miss method of guess, conjecture and mother-wit. That period of catch-as-catch can economic action has passed with everybody with a grain of common sense, except the Honorable Black Kluxer [Marcus Garvey]. Thus, it ought to be apparent that the right to criticize work or upon the fact of having done it. Hence, it is the sheerest idle prattle and an evidence of dishonesty and guilt for Garvey to retort to persons who charge him with shamelessly mishandling the Black Star Line that they are not pilots or captains, that they have owned and operated no ship lines, and, consequently are not justified in criticizing him! Of course, he, naturally, would wish that to be so. It is the stock and trade of crooks to call others crooks who condemn them. *It is always to the interest of a man with a false stone to impeach the knowledge and honor of a lapidary.* That is the only way he can defraud the public. By lying about Owen's and Randolph's business ability, Garvey thinks that he will be able to divert attention from his own appalling business ignorance and tricks. But he has another thought coming.

Listen to this grandiose balderdash and burlesque on business. Speaking of what *he* has done, with emphasis on "he," if you please—he says that he has established the greatest Negro paper—the *Negro World*. That is a lie. The *Chicago Defender* is, by long odds, the greatest Negro paper in the world. Every honest, intelligent Negro knows that. What sort of newspaper is the *Negro World*, anyway, which devotes its front page, the news page of every modern, civilized, recognized newspaper in newspaperdom, to the wild vaporings, imbecile puerilities and arrant nonsense, of a consummate ignoramus? But what's claiming the greatest Negro newspaper in the world, or the greatest anything in the world, to this Supreme and Exalted Ruler of the Annanias fraternity?

On his erratic rampage of mendacity and bigoted, groundless braggadocio, he beats the air, waving his big, fat hands furiously, and yaps: "We find established to the credit of the Negro a line of steam ships known as the Black Star Line, which has sent out two of its ships on the high seas and has registered the Negro as a competitor in maritime affairs." Is that so? And to the credit of the Negro! Can you beat that for unmitigated, arrogant asininity?

## 2. A Union Revolution

### a. Randolph Describes the Fight with the Pullman Company
Extract from: A. Philip Randolph, "Porters Get Inside Data on Wage Tilt: Organizer of Union Outlines Fight," *Chicago Defender* (19 November 1927): 1, 10. Reprinted with permission of the *Chicago Defender*.

Randolph described an early and important battle with the Pullman Company. Pullman officials tried to use the federal government's mediation machinery to its advantage. The Brotherhood of Sleeping Car Porters objected strenuously, and Randolph used this article to expose Pullman's tactics and to drum up support for the union's efforts.

> Through two eventful years one of the most heroic and historic fights ever waged in America has been waged against one of America's most powerful industrial monarchs, the Pullman Company, by black men, the heirs of former slaves.
>
> In August, 1925, a few brave, bold black men, undaunted and unafraid, fired by the vision of a brighter day of economic justice, hurled their organized hosts in the sacred name of truth righteousness against the Pullman Company's despotic company union, known as the employees' representation plan, which is company organized, company owned and company controlled. . . .
>
> *Form Brotherhood*
> And who were these men? Who began this union? Contrary to the childish charge, they were not blacksmiths, carpenters, preachers, lawyers, anarchists, communists, nurses or doctors, but insiders—men in the Pullman service, running on the road. It is they who built, supported and maintained the organization and made it possible for the brotherhood to present the porters' case to the United States mediation board in preliminary hearings December 10 and in subsequent hearings July 11 in the Congress hotel, Chicago, Ill.
>
> In those hearings Hon. Edwin [sic] P. Morrow of the United States mediation board determined whether the brotherhood's case deserved investigation or not, or whether it was the idle vaporings of some irresponsible enthusiasts. In those hearings the representatives of the brotherhood presented the membership of the union to establish its right to represent the porters and maids. In reply the company offered in evidence the results of the election under the employees' representation plan, wherein the company contended that 85 per cent of the porters and maids had voted for the plan.
>
> Against the company's claim, the brotherhood offered 1,000 affidavits to prove that the porters did not vote of their own free will, that they were not

free agents, but voted under intimidation and coercion, which the brotherhood contended was a flagrant violation of the railway labor act.

The Pullman Company also contended that it had a contract with its employees. The brotherhood answered that the alleged contract was fraudulent, null and void, and could not be validated in a court of law, since it was made under duress, wherein there was not a valid meeting of minds of free agents, but that it could be compared to a contract signed on the dotted line by a man at the point of a revolver. In which instance the man does not sign said contract because he wants to, but because he felt that he had to in order to save his job. Such a contract will and ought to be broken as soon as the intimidated party to it receives the power to break it. The law no more recognizes the right of a man to be intimidated to sign away his rights than it recognizes the right of a man to sign away his life. Such a public policy would destroy the stability and security of property. Nor does the law recognize the right of a man to commit suicide, or to commit arson and burn down his house within an organized community, or to testify against himself. As a public agent his acts must be regulated by the public's interests.

The contract claimed by the company under the plan was made by the company with itself, which cannot hold under the law. A man cannot make a contract with himself for such a contract would not constitute the required meeting of minds, but only the action of one mind. It would have no meaning or force in a court of law....

*Smoke Screen Contract*

What is the significance of this? Just this. The counterfeit contract which two of the most prominent delegates to the last company union wage conference, Messrs. Bennie Smith of Omaha and Edwards of St. Louis, refused to sign, was used as a smoke screen to conceal the company's insolent defiance of the Railway Labor Act by flatly refusing to arbitrate the dispute.

In an effort to evade and confuse the issue, L. S. Hungerford, vice present and general manager of the Pullman Company, contended that there was no dispute. But, on the contrary, the United States mediation board said there was a dispute. Mr. Hungerford also said the porters didn't want any organization as shown by the fact that they tried to organize two or three times before and failed, as though this was any good reason why porters did not want to organize now.

The brotherhood's representatives answered that that was no reason why the porters did not want organized now. Mr. Hungerford also contended that the porters wanted the plan because they voted for it. Whereupon Mr. Morrow replied, "All right, Mr. Hungerford, if you think your position is correct, that your statements about the porters' wishes are true, why not present them to a board of arbitration. The United States mediation board will see to it that you get an honest, fair and responsible board which will confirm your position if you are right, and it will set you right if you are wrong." This was certainly a fair proposition, but the company rejected it. Why?

There are several reasons. The company knew that its case would not bear examination, that the brotherhood surely would win and that several millions of dollars would be added to the pay roll for the porters, that its notoriously unfair dealings with the porters would be exposed to the public. The company also felt that if it refused to arbitrate such action would demoralize the union and shoot it to pieces, that the porters would throw up their hands in despair and refuse to go further. But, of course, the company was wrong again.

In refusing to arbitrate the dispute, the company was in the same position as a man with a phony diamond. When he offered it for sale as a genuine diamond and the prospective buyer said that he wouldn't buy it until it was submitted to a lapidary, an expert on stones, the seller said, oh no, if you won't buy it until I submit it to an expert on stones to determine whether it is a genuine diamond as I say it is then I won't sell it; or like the violinist who claimed that he was the finest violinist in the world, but when requested to play, refused, proving that his playing would stand anything but being heard; or a painter whose picture would stand anything but being seen. So the Pullman Company's alleged contract, its statements and claims about the wishes of the porters, will stand anything but being examined. . . .

*Wins Victory*

The company didn't have sufficient faith in its brains and ability to trick the brotherhood into writing an agreement for the benefit of the company only. It's interesting to note that the company is forever holding bogus wage conferences under the plan composed of its handpicked Uncle Toms, who are conveniently juggled and manipulated at will to suit the company's purposes. The company union delegates to wage conferences neither have the knowledge or the freedom and power necessary to write a sound and sensible contract. That is why the company will hold conferences with them.

The brotherhood won a victory when it forced the company to take a position on arbitration. Although the company agreed to the Watson-Parker bill, which planned that arbitration should automatically follow mediation, in the event that mediation failed, it balked when the porters raised the question of arbitration. For when it agreed to arbitration in the Railway Labor Act, doubtless, the company never dreamed that some day that same ghost of arbitration would plague it in the form of a bona fide porters' union demanding arbitration. By every principle, strategy and precedent of labor organization in the transportation industry the fight between the brotherhood and the Pullman Company should have ended when the case reached arbitration. Such has been the case with other railroad unions and carriers under the Railway Labor Act. But the Pullman Company violated the spirit and intent of the act by attempting to hide behind a technicality; namely, its right to refuse to arbitrate, although it is now arbitrating the case with its Pullman conductors, who are white. This is rank and indefensible discrimination.

The brotherhood's program now is to create an emergency which will require the United States mediation board to recommend to the president of the United States that he appoint an emergency board to inquire into this whole dispute between the brotherhood and the Pullman Company. Under the Railway Labor Act there are three stages through which a dispute between employees and the carrier may go: (1) mediation, (2) arbitration, (3) the emergency board. When a dispute is not settled by the first two stages then said dispute may be investigated by an emergency board if it has assumed the aspect of an emergency or a threat of interrupting interstate commerce. The law provides that the emergency board shall inquire into the dispute for 30 days and then report its findings which are calculated to remove the emergency and prevent a probable interruption of interstate commerce.

Another angle of action the brotherhood is adopting is the presentation of its case to the Interstate Commerce Commission, with a view to securing an investigation of the rates of the Pullman Company in relation to wages and working conditions. The brotherhood's petition was answered by the company and the answer of the company has, in turn, been answered by the brotherhood. The company contended that the Interstate Commerce Commission has no jurisdiction since the brotherhood seeks to raise wages, and that another arm of the government, the Railway Labor Act, has been set up to handle such matters. Here, the company is in a dilemma, because the company seeks to hide behind the very railway labor which it notoriously defied and refused to abide by when it took the position of not accepting arbitration urged and recommended upon it by Edwin [sic] P. Morrow of the United States mediation board.

The company is in utter confusion and uncertainty. At one time it denied the law, and when pressed to cover, seeks to hide behind that very law in order to avoid investigation by the Interstate Commerce Commission. Of course the Pullman Company's is as unsound as it is insincere. The brotherhood's answer has cut the ground from under the company and exposed it naked to the public.

*Confusion Reigns*

The company is now conducting elections under the employees' representation plan. It is compelling the porters to vote in order to be able to say that the porters have voted for the plan, the company union. It is threatening to pull porters off their line and even fire them if they refuse to swallow the plan—hook, line and sinker. It is also compelling porters to sign a petition under threat of firing them, to the effect that they, the porters, renounce the Brotherhood of Sleeping Car Porters and remain loyal to the plan. A large number of the porters are refusing to sign these petitions, and those who have signed are signing affidavits to the effect that they signed under intimidation and coercion to protect their jobs, but that they want the brotherhood to represent them in the making of agreements on wages, rules and working condition with the Pullman Company. Despite the unlawful intimidation being practiced by the company upon the porters in order to compel them, the porters, to act against their own interests, the porters are standing firm. They are paying their dues and assessments, and in meetings from coast to coast have resolutely signified their intention to go to the limit with their fight to secure a living wage, better working conditions and manhood rights. The public has shown, by the unanimous favorable reporting of the porters' case filed with the Interstate Commerce Commission in the nation's press, dailies and weeklies, that it is on the side of the porters, for $72 a month in wages and 40 hours of work, under obviously unfair working conditions, and the dependence of porters, whose labor earned for the company more than $20,000,000 in net profits in 1926, upon professional begging in the form of receiving tips for a living would not be countenanced by an enlightened public.

## b. The *Chicago Defender* lends its support to the Brotherhood of Sleeping Car Porters

Extract from: "The Pullman Porters' Organization," *Chicago Defender* (19 November 1927): pt. 2, p. 2. Reprinted with permission of the *Chicago Defender*.

Randolph had a difficult time in eliciting the support of some elements in the black community. In particular, he struggled to gain the respect of several key black newspapers such as the *Pittsburgh Courier* and the *Chicago Defender*. In this article, the editors of the *Chicago Defender* announced that they in fact supported the BSCP.

> There has been considerable criticism pro and con [on] the so-called attitude of the Defender on the movement to organize the Pullman porters and maids. It is felt and asserted by some that the Defender is opposed to the porters' efforts at organization. It is alleged that the Defender has not given proper space to the Brotherhood of Sleeping Car Porters side of the fight.
>
> Whatever may be the merits of these charges, be it known by all whom it may concern that the Defender is a red-blooded four-square Race paper, which is unequivocally committed to the policy of supporting all bona fide Race movements. Therefore, we wish definitely to register the fact that we back and favor the right of the Pullman porters and maids to organize into a bona fide union of their own choosing, untrammeled by the Pullman Company.
>
> After a careful survey and review of the determined and lawful struggle of the Pullman porters, led by the brilliant and fearless A. Philip Randolph over

a period of two years, the Defender herewith announces its determination to fight with the porters, arm in arm, shoulder to shoulder, for a living wage and better working conditions.

It is a notorious fact that $72.50 a month is entirely inadequate to maintain a family according to decent American standards of living.

It is also indefensible for the Pullman Company to allege that the meager wage is subsidized by tips. No porter can budget his home expenses on tips he has not received. Nor can any porter predict the amount of tips he will receive any month, since he may be deadheaded around the country at any time, in which event he receives no tips, because no one is on the car but himself. Besides, no porter can maintain his sense of self-respect who is required to beg the public for a handout in the form of tips. Any work, regardless of race or color, who renders a fair day's work is entitled to a fair day's wage.

The Defender also regards the practice of the Pullman Company requiring porters to work hours known as preparatory time without pay as an outrage which no fair-minded American can countenance. The porters and maids are entitled to the same regulation transportation work month of 240 hours as other railway employees enjoy, and pay as overtime for every hour over 240.

It is the hope of the defender that the Pullman Company, a national utility, will realize its obligation to meet in conference the porters' own representatives as selected by them without intimidation or coercion.

Porters are responsible for the rapid and tremendous growth of the Pullman Company and are naturally deserving of a just consideration.

It is obviously unfair for the company to refuse to recognize and meet in conference the porters' union but to recognize and deal with the conductors' union. We cannot believe that the company will persist in this undemocratic and un-American attitude. According to the statement of Hon. Edwin [sic] P. Morrow, the Pullman Company and the Brotherhood of Sleeping Car Porters were urged to arbitrate their dispute. The brotherhood agreed, but the company refused, but is now arbitrating the case with the conductors. On account of this attitude the porters' union has been compelled to seek relief from the interstate commerce commission and the emergency board.

We feel that the Pullman Company may salvage some of its lost public good will if it will accept the inevitable situation and recognize the brotherhood and proceed to writing an agreement on wages, rules and working conditions, for the employee representation plan or company union will continue to be the source of endless discontent among the porters, which can only result in demoralizing the morale of the men and thereby lower the standard of working efficiency. Satisfied workers mean higher standards of work; higher standards of work mean more profits.

The Defender, therefore, takes the side of the porters' fight to organize for their rights as other workers have done and we bid them Godspeed.

## c. The *Pittsburgh Courier* Opposes the Brotherhood of Sleeping Car Porters

Extract from: "Calling a Halt (by a Pullman Porter)," *Pittsburgh Courier* (5 May 1928): sec. 2, p. 8. Reprinted with the permission of GRM Associates, Inc., agents for the *Pittsburgh Courier*.

While battling the Pullman Company, Randolph lost the backing of the influential African American newspaper, the *Pittsburgh Courier*, whose editor, Robert L. Vann, began publishing anti-BSCP articles and editorials in the late 1920s. Below is an example of an anti-Randolph editorial.

To the editors of the New York Age and Pittsburgh Courier:

If the readers of the Age will excuse my digression I should like to acknowledge my appreciation of the fairness on the part of the editor of The Courier in his attempt to show Randolph his error.

The Pullman Company will not recognize the so-called Brotherhood of Sleeping Car Porters with Randolph at the head of it, nor out of it so there need be no more worry on that point.

The fact of the matter is, that the organization does not represent the porters and since the porters have not organized it nor approached the Pullman Company, the Pullman Company has no cause to recognize them. I recently wrote the manager and questioned the right of the company to recognize that so-called Brotherhood either by bargaining with them or bringing pressure to bear on the porter in service. There can be no legitimate organization unless the porters are represented in the election of officers and in formulating the plans of procedure, this has been the done and therefore the porter cannot be lawfully represented. There are a vast number of porters, including myself, who would not stand for the recognition, without protest even if the company wanted to do so and this is right from the shoulder, so before there is any fight for the company to take up we who are supposed to be in the minority group, demand of Randolph or anyone, something to say and be heard on the subject which concerns us more than it does those that are so outspoken.

I think the Negro press in general has gone just a mite too far with Randolph without knowing the facts and yet when there was no voice to be heard but Randolph's there is some excuse. The Pullman Company would not say anything because they did not think it worth their while and every Negro paper that had the wisdom to see and courage to say, was supposed to be bought in by the Pullman Company. As a matter of fact, I don't believe the company has ever paid a penny to any Negro edition to fight this propaganda and I certainly don't believe they ever offered Randolph a penny.

Be that as it may, however, the job belongs to me and 25,000 other Negroes and Randolph or anyone else may as well look for another job if they expect to make their living by driving us out into the field of unemployment and until that point is settled the Pullman Company is not licked because they have no cause to enter the fight. It is true that most of our porters are unlearned and don't think much and are therefore easy prey for a man of Randolph's type, who can show the imaginary wrong and magnify it, but there are enough of us I am sure to protect the job that has been the heritage of the race for more than 60 years, so we call upon the Negro press to keep quiet on the subject or deal with the facts.

The Negro press is supported and maintained by Negro patronage which is made possible by the consideration of the value of the Negro laborer by capital, resulting in employment and the Pullman Company stands alone as the greatest benefactor to Negro advancement. The labor organization (white) has never played a card (knowingly) intended to benefit the race. In fact, since the laborer is the most ignorant of the population we may justly assume that all race hatred and discrimination is born in the labor group then why have they become so loving all of a sudden.

D. D. Watson<br>
607 Shawmut Avenue,<br>
Boston, Mass.

## d. Robert L. Vann Argues Against Unions

Extract from: Robert L. Vann, "The Camera," *Pittsburgh Courier* (12 May 1928), sec. 1, p. 1. Reprinted with the permission of GRM Associates, Inc., agents for the *Pittsburgh Courier*.

In this article, Robert L. Vann attacks the idea that African American workers should join labor unions. His intent is to undercut Randolph's efforts with the porters and in the labor movement generally.

The Pittsburgh Courier offers no apology for any support its gives Negro movements in this country. We believe it to be the policy of every well-regulated Negro journal to espouse the course of the colored man of this country. The greatest good for the greatest number ought to be the program; and while there may be exceptions to be found, the general rule, we think, is a safe one.

As between capital and labor in this country: Let it be known that it has always been the policy of The Courier to cultivate a friendly feeling between the colored working man in this country and American capital. Labor unions may be all right for white men—and there are times when we doubt their efficiency even for white men; but so far as the American Negro is concerned, the labor unions offer him no hope. As between the union and American capital the colored man ought to be able to choose capital without the slightest hesitation. The labor unions not only fight the colored man to keep him out of the unions, except in rare and inconsequential instances, but they fight to keep him and capital apart so that the colored man profits nothing by forming a union, but loses the possibility of a profitable contract with capital. It is all a question of bread and butter; and the colored man in this country who earns his bread and butter by the sweat of his brow must remember that capital is his employer, and if he serves capital efficiently capital is also his friend. It seems to us futile argument for labor to urge colored men to form unions of their own for the purpose of fighting capital when the labor unions refuse to accept Negroes as a general proposition and yet raise an awful howl if Negroes accept positions in open shops. The Negro must learn to make his own bargain with capital: earn his own pay envelope; and at least for the present let the labor unions do the fighting. When labor unions are ready to share the economic problems of the country with the colored worker it will be plenty of time for the colored man to make application for membership. We do not expect this condition to prevail for some decades to come.

## 3. When Negroes Don't March

### a. Randolph Calls for a March on Washington

Extract from: A. Philip Randolph, "Let the Negro Masses Speak." *The Black Worker* 7, no. 3 (March 1941): 4. Reprinted with permission from the A. Philip Randolph Institute.

Well before the United States formally entered World War II, A. Philip Randolph was protesting discrimination in President Franklin D. Roosevelt's efforts to shore up the nation's defenses. In this article, Randolph boldly states his views that black workers ought to have the right to work in defense factories.

> Negroes have a stake in National Defense. It is a big stake. It is a vital and important stake.
> But are we getting our stake?
> No. Nobody cares anything about us. We are being pushed around.
> The stake involves jobs. It involves equal employment opportunities. It involves equal opportunity for integration in the armed forces of the nation.
> And what do we get?
> Polite promises; sometimes, insults. How can this stake be protected?
> Our answer is:
> Let the Negro masses speak!
> Yet. Thirteen or fifteen million Negroes have a stake of far-reaching economic consequence sin the Government's expenditure of twenty, or more, billions for National Defense.

Negroes have a stake in the vast nation-wide, Government program of vocational training of workers to perform skilled work on contracts to produce munitions and build all types of ships for war.

How can Negroes win their right to equal opportunities to share in this plan of training and retraining for technical services?

Our answer is:

Let the Negro masses speak!

Negroes must not fail to grasp and understand the fact that National Defense is not an ordinary, passing event. They must realize that this world-war crisis is not a temporary, simple, occasional incident.

The world-war crisis and America's scheme of National Defense are destined profoundly to affect the whole economy of our country. Sharp and permanent rearrangements and readjustments in the entire industrial and work setups of business, industry and labor are in the process of development.

If the Negro is shut out of these extensive and intensive changes in industry, labor and business, the race will be set back over fifty years.

Indeed, it is seriously doubtful that if the Negro waits until these economic, trade union and business transformations and innovations, now under way, under the sanction and guidance of the Government, are crystallized and yet he may never retrieve lost ground or salvage rights sacrificed.

How can the Negro halt this crystallization of economic and political injustice?

Our answer is:

Let the Negro masses speak!

When they speak, they will speak with the tongues of angels. When they thunder their resentment and revolt against the blighting bottlenecks of race prejudice and hatreds, *their voice will be the Voice of God.*

How shall they speak?

Let us not be beaten, bewildered and bitter. Away with cynicism and defeatism.

Let the Negro masses speak with ten thousand Negroes strong, marching down Pennsylvania Avenue in the Capitol of the Nation, singing "John Brown's Body Lies a 'Mouldering [sic] in the Grave'" and "Before I'll Be a Slave, I'll Be Buried in My Grave and Go Home to My Father and Be Saved."

In serried ranks, let the Negro masses, as workers, doctors, preachers, lawyers, businessmen, nurses, teachers, women and children, march forward with heads erect, holding banners aloft, inscribed with slogans, preaching the gospel of justice, freedom and democracy, declaring their decisive demands for jobs in National Defense, equal employment and vocational training opportunities, together with equal privileges for integration in all departments of the armed forces.

Let us tear the mask of hypocrisy from America's Democracy!

An able expose of discrimination against Negroes on National Defense jobs was made by Walter White, Secretary of the National Association for the Advancement of Colored People in the *Saturday Evening Post*, of recent date, and now Negroes must mobilize their might to stop it.

Negroes cannot stop discrimination in National Defense with conferences of leaders and the intelligentsia alone. While conferences have merit, they won't get desired results by themselves.

During the first world's war immigration from Europe was cut off and labor was at a premium. Hundreds of thousands of Negroes were brought up from the South to labor in the factories, mines and mils. They were needed badly. Jobs were seeking them.

Today, it is different. During this World War, there are millions of workers in America unemployed. White workers are in sharp competition now with Negro workers for jobs. Instead of jobs seeking workers, workers are seeking jobs.

Therefore, whatever Negroes get in jobs and vocational training opportunities, they must fight for. Nothing will be given them.

Hence, let the Negroes masses speak!

Let the Negro masses march!

Let the Negro masses fight!

When women marched in demonstration in England and America, they won the ballot.

When the American Legions marched on Washington, they secured the bonus.

Let no black man be afraid! We are simply fighting for our constitutional rights as American citizens.

We are not saboteurs.

We are no Quislings.

We hold no allegiance to an alien state. This is our own, our native land. Let us fight to make it truly free, democratic and just.

We are not Trojan Horses.

We are not Fifth Columnists.

We are not traitors.

We are Americans.

We are patriots.

We are fighting for the right to work!

We are fighting for the right to live!

We believe in National Unity.

We believe in National Defense.

We will fight for Uncle Sam!

We are opposed to totalitarian tyranny, Fascist, Nazi and Communist.

We will fight for democracy!

Yes, we will fight!

Indeed, we would rather die on our feet fighting for Negroes' rights than to live on our knees as half-men; as semi-citizens, begging for a pittance.

Therefore, let the Negro masses speak!
Let the Negro masses march!
On to Washington, ten thousand black Americans!

Let them swarm from every hamlet, village and town; from the highways and byways, out of the churches, lodges, homes, schools, mills, mines; factories and fields. Let them come in automobiles, buses, trains, trucks and on feet. Let them come though the winds blow and the rains beat against them, when the date is set.

We call not upon our white friends to march with us. There are some things Negroes must do alone. This is our fight and we must see it through.

If it costs money to finance a march on Washington, let Negroes pay for it. If any sacrifices are to be made for Negro rights in National Defense, let Negroes make them.

If Negroes fail this chance for work, for freedom and training, it may never come again.

Let the Negro masses speak!

Only the masses possess power. Only the voice of the masses will be heard and heeded—Negro America has never yet spoken as a mass; an organized mass.

Top powers of industry, organized white labor and government, have not yet felt the pressure of the Negro masses. They have seen Negro leaders, leaders who are intelligent and well-meaning, pleading for Negro rights.

They have never seen the Negro masses in action.

Thus, let the Negro masses speak!

## b. Executive Order 8802 Reaffirming Policy Of Full Participation In The Defense Program By All Persons, Regardless Of Race, Creed, Color, Or National Origin, And Directing Certain Action In Furtherance Of Said Policy
Extract from: *Federal Register* 6, no. 125 (27 June 1941): 4544.

Hailed by many civil rights leaders as the second Emancipation Proclamation, the issuance of Executive Order 8802 remains one of Randolph's greatest achievements. The presidential order outlawed discrimination in hiring for defense contractors and the federal government for the duration of the war.

> WHEREAS it is the policy of the United States to encourage full participation in the national defense program by all citizens of the United States, regardless of race, creed, color, or national origin, in the firm belief that the democratic way of life within the Nation can be defended successfully only with the help and support of all groups within its borders; and

WHEREAS there is evidence that available and needed workers have been barred from employment in industries engaged in defense production solely because of considerations of race, creed, color, or national origin, to the detriment of workers' morale and of national unity:

NOW, THEREFORE, by virtue of the authority vested in me by the Constitution and the statutes, and as a prerequisite to the successful conduct of our national defense production effort, I do hereby reaffirm the policy of the United States that there shall be no discrimination in the employment of workers in defense industries or government because of race, creed, color, or national origin, and I do hereby declare that it is the duty of employers and of labor organizations, in furtherance of said policy and of this order, to provide for the full and equitable participation of all workers in defense industries, without discrimination because of race, creed, color, or national origin;

And it is hereby ordered as follows:

1. All departments and agencies of the Government of the United States concerned with vocational and training programs for defense production shall take special measures appropriate to assure that such programs are administered without discrimination because of race, creed, color, or national origin;

2. All contracting agencies of the Government of the United States shall include in all defense contracts hereafter negotiated by them a provision obligating the contractor not to discriminate against any worker because of race, creed, color, or national origin;

3. There is established in the Office of Production Management a Committee on Fair Employment Practice, which shall consist of a chairman and four other members to be appointed by the President. The Chairman and members of the Committee shall serve as such without compensation but shall be entitled to actual and necessary transportation, subsistence and other expenses incidental to performance of their duties. The Committee shall receive and investigate complaints of discrimination in violation of the provisions of this order and shall take appropriate steps to redress grievances which it finds to be valid. The Committee shall also recommend to the several departments and agencies of the Government of the United States and to the President all measures which may be deemed by it necessary or proper to effectuate the provisions of this order.

Franklin D. Roosevelt
The White House
June 25, 1941

## c. Randolph Explains Why He Postponed the 1941 March on Washington

Extract from: A. Philip Randolph, "Why and How the March Was Postponed." *Black Worker* 7, no. 8 (August 1941): 1–2. Reprinted with permission from the A. Philip Randolph Institute.

In exchange for President Franklin D. Roosevelt's Executive Order 8802, Randolph promised to call off his proposed 1941 March on Washington. Not all civil rights activists appreciated Randolph's bargain. In this article, Randolph defends himself against his critics.

Briefly, why the March? The March on Washington was the last resort of a desperate people who had failed to get decisive results in the form of jobs in National Defense through conferences, petitions and appeals to leaders of government and private industry.

Conferences had been held with the President, Secretary of the Army, Henry L. Stimson, Secretary of the Navy, Frank Knox, Co-Director of the Office of Production Management Sidney Hillman, National Direction of the National Youth Administration, Aubrey Williams, Mayor LaGuardia and many others by Walter White, Mary McLeod Bethune, Dr. Channing H. Tobias, Lester Granger, Dr. F. D. Patterson, Dr. Rayford H. Logan, T. Arnold Hill, George Goodman, Will Alexander, Judge William H. Hastie, Dr. Robert C. Weaver, and others. In these conferences, government leaders were genial, gracious and reassuring of their opposition to discrimination on account of race, color, creed or national origin. But Negroes got no jobs.

As a result of the failure of these conferences by honest, able and courageous Negro leaders, the idea of the March-on-Washington was conceived by the writer. Articles on the proposed march were written and sent to the Negro press. Happily, the press, that is the Negro press—I add this emphasis because the white press maintained a dreadful conspiracy of silence on the March idea—received the plan for Negroes to March-on-Washington for jobs and justice in National Defense with an open mind and gave it general support, with the exception of the Pittsburgh Courier which opposed the March editorially, although carrying new releases on it.

*White Press*

Here is one exception with the white daily press. It is "P.M." This paper promptly championed the March idea.

While the March-on-Washington was being discussed in the Negro press, "P.M." had waged a vigorous fight in page after page for the right of Negroes to jobs in National Defense.

Soon the movement to March-on-Washington captured the imagination of the Negroes all over the country and spread like a prairie fire.

No section of the Negro people refused to respond to the "Call" to Negro America to mobilize 100,000 strong to March-on-Washington for jobs in National Defense. Negro preachers, doctors, lawyers, teachers, students, youth, laborers, trade unionists, women, children, businessmen, editors, reporters, artists, soldiers, yes, Negro America of every stratum, calling and endeavor, rallied to the new adventure in Negro mass action for jobs and dignity.

Never, verily, had Negroes of hand and brain been so deeply stirred before to struggle for their rights. And they struggled together.

But white America was unaware of these stirrings of the Negro for new economic opportunities. The press and radio were silent.

Meanwhile, an avalanche of Negro discontent and resentment to discriminations was rolling up and gathering a telling and threatening force and the March-on-Washington was rapidly taking on the character of a crusade.

*Negro Unity*

It is significant of racial solidarity that the National Negro Women's Council had been called to meet in Washington, D.C., by its leader, Mrs. Mary McLeod [Bethune], one day before the March. And the NAACP, one of the leading exponents of the March, cut short its National Conference one day to permit its delegates to participate in the March. The New England Convention of Negro Baptist Preachers endorsed the March and demonstrated its spirit by singing "Onward Christian Soldiers, Marching As To War," following a talk by the National Director of the March. Mount Oliver Baptist Church of New York upon an appeal by the National Director and O. Clay Maxwell, its able Pastor, collected one hundred fourteen dollars and forty cents ($114.40) and contributed it to the March.

*Official Washington Concerned*

But no apparent concern had been manifested about the March by Government leaders, until the National Director addressed a letter to President Roosevelt, requesting him to speak to the Marchers at the Monument of Abraham Lincoln following the March, July 1st. Letters were also addressed to Secretary of War Stimson and of the Navy, Knox, Knudsen and Hillman, Co-Directors of the OPM, Secretary of Labor Perkins, Mayor LaGuardia and Mrs. Roosevelt, requesting them to speak to the Negro Marchers.

Shortly following the sending of these letters, the National Director and Walter White were called for conferences with Mrs. Roosevelt and Mayor LaGuardia. They were urged to call off the March, expressing fears that the March would harm the Negro. Their requests were refused.

*White House Conference*

Later a conference was called at the White House by President Roosevelt in which sat Walter White, Frank R. Crosswaith, Chairman of the Negro Labor Committee of Harlem, Layle Lane, Vice-President of the American Federation of Teachers and the Writer.

The whole question of the March-on-Washington was discussed by the President, Secretary of War Stimson, Secretary of the Navy Knox, Mayor LaGuardia, Hillman and Knudsen, Anna Rosenberg of the Social Security Board and Aubrey Williams of N.Y.A. Following the conference with the President, he ordered these heads of the departments of Government to find a remedy for this problem of discrimination on account of race, color, creed or national origin in National Defense. This White House conference was held on June 18th and the President issued the famous Executive Order, June 25, despite strenuous opposition from some powerful department heads.

*Executive Order*

When the Executive Order was issued, the National Director called up Walter White of the NAACP, in Houston, Texas, and placed the matter before him and he expressed his agreement to postponement. He then called Henry K. Craft of the Harlem YMCA, in New York City, and he indicated his agreement to postponement. Mr. Craft was also requested to contact other members of the National Negro March-on-Washington Committee to get their decision on the question of postponing the March in view of the issuance of the Executive Order, the main objective of the March-on-Washington. All of the members reached agreed to postponement. Two of the members of the Committee, Rev. A. Clayton Powell, Jr., and Richard Parish, Chairman of the Youth Division, have opposed postponement.

*Why March Postponed?*

Simply stated, the March was postponed because its main objective, namely, the issuance of an Executive Order banning discrimination in National Defense, was secured in conference with the President.

What about discrimination in the departments of the Federal Government? This is one of our objectives. While it is one of our objectives, it was not our main objective. We consider that it is much more important to get jobs for Negroes in National Defense, than to get them in the Army or Navy or Air Corps, although we shall continue to fight to abolish discriminations on account of race, color, creed or national origin in all departments of the government and the armed forces of the nation. This will be the next step in the fight of the Negro March-on-Washington movement.

The National Negro March-on-Washington Committee would have been placed in an untenable, absurd, and ridiculous position had it rejected its chief objective when offered by the President on the grounds that we didn't get everything we wanted as a pretext for Marching-on-Washington anyhow.

*Example of Organized Labor*

One needs but a cursory knowledge of the history of the struggles of organized labor and its tactics and strategy to understand that no maneuver of organized labor of the mass action of a minority people wins all of its demands. Nor is the fight carried out of the conference room to the streets unless its major demand is rejected.

Witness the tactic of the strike as a weapon of the trade union to achieve recognition of the union, higher wages and better working conditions.

The policy of the trade union is first to seek to settle the dispute in conference with the employer. Failing in this effort a strike vote is taken as an expression of the will and spirit of the workers and a date for the strike is set. Conference is sought again either by the trade union or the employer to seek and attempt an adjustment of the basic points of difference. It may or may not succeed. If the fundamental demand of the union is refused, the strike, assuming that conditions are favorable, will be called. But if the primary aim of the Organization is granted, the strike is called off.

*Tactics of the Strike*

Probably, thousands of strike votes are taken yearly, but only a small fraction of strikes for which the votes were taken are ever actually called. It would be silly and suicidal folly and disastrous to a trade union to make demands upon the employer, win the principal ones in conference and yet call the strike anyway in order to satisfy some so-called revolutionary, radical or extremist whims of some of its members.

The transport Workers Union of New York recently took a strike vote and set the date for the strike on the subway system. Certain demands were made to the Mayor and the Board of Transportation of New York City. In conference some of these demands were realized and the strike was called off.

About a year ago, twenty-one (21) standard Railroad unions took a strike vote for two weeks' vacation with pay. The Railway carriers have not yet granted this demand, but no strike has been called.

However, when C.I.O. made its demand for recognition upon "Little Steel," and it was rejected, strikes were called. There was no other alternative. When C.I.O. made its demand for recognition upon "Big Steel"—United States Steel Corporation, and received it, resort was made to the method and technique of the conference table and no strike occurred.

This same principle of action obtains in the domain of mass movements. In the case of the Negro March-on-Washington Program, the issuance of the Executive Order by the President was made upon the condition that the March be called off.

In the face of this significant achievement, the March could not with reason and sanity be carried on unless the main purpose of the movement was to *march for the sake of the march and not to get jobs for the Negro masses.*

If the purpose of the Negro March-on-Washington movement had been to march regardless of any action the President might make to break down discriminations in National Defense, it would not be worthy of the confidence and support of the Negro masses.

The philosophy back of the March-on-Washington is not that the March is an end in itself. On the contrary, it is a means to an end, the end being the economic improvement of the Negro people by the breaking down of barriers in National Defense in order that Negro workers may get jobs on which they may make wages, with which they buy food, clothing and shelter, the basis of life.

Therefore, I want to make it clear, that the purpose of the March-on-Washington movement was not to serve as an agency to create a continuing state of sullen unrest and blind resentment among Negroes against discriminations. There is sufficient of this. Its purpose was and is to achieve a specific and definite thing, namely, elimination of barriers to jobs for Negroes. It would have constituted a definite betrayal of the interests of the Negro masses if the National Negro March-on-Washington Committee after receiving from the President the main object of its struggle, the Executive Order, had defiantly waved it aside and marched on Washington. Such strategy would have promptly and rightly been branded as a lamentable specie of infantile leftism and an appeal to sheer prima donna dramatics and heroics.

*Nature of Mass Action*
Moreover, the objectives of the March-on-Washington were simple and possible of immediate attainment. Without an issue which is clear, understandable and possible of realization, the masses cannot be rallied. The masses cannot comprehend and will not respond to an omnibus program with a multiplicity of aims or abstract ideologies. The leaders of the March-on-Washington knew this.

*Spiritual Movement*
While the March-on-Washington had positive and practical aims, it was and is fundamentally spiritual and moral in content and implications. It is the first demonstration on a national scale of the faith of the Negro people in themselves, in their own capacity to win their rights against opposition. Those of us who had the privilege to play some part in it have a solemn responsibility, obligation and duty to remain true to that faith of the Negro masses. This means that those who are guiding it must subordinate their own interests and future to the interest and future of the Negro people.

# 4. Unfinished Business

### a. Randolph's Ideas for a New Political Party
Extract from: "Ideas for A New Party: Provisional Declaration of Principles of the National Educational Committee for a New Party," *The Antioch Review* 6 (Fall 1946): 449–50, 470–72. Copyright © 1946 by the Antioch Review, Inc. (renewed 1973). First appeared in the *Antioch Review* 6, no. 3. Reprinted with permission of the editors.

After the death of Franklin D. Roosevelt in 1945, some liberals and Leftists felt that the Democratic Party no longer represented their interests. In this article, Randolph and his colleagues on the National Educational Committee for a New Party proposed a broad outline of a new political party that would take up the central issues of liberalism including civil rights, full employment, health care, and education.

> The American people need a new political alignment and policy to secure satisfaction of their urgent economic, political and social wants, in a world where pressing inescapable problems call for progressive answers.
>
> The Republican and Democratic parties demonstrate an increasing inability to meet these wants. Liberals in the Republican party are frustrated while the New Deal is a spent force in the Democratic party.
>
> A never-ending danger is present in the bi-partisan Congressional coalition of reactionary Democrats and Republicans. Progressive measures are adopted against the coalition's savage opposition. The coalition prevented adoption of legislation for fully effective reconversion and price control, for measures to encourage full employment and for fair employment practices, for an adequate housing program that is so needed by the American people. It has prevented adoption of anti-discrimination laws while crackpot groups inflame the racial and religious hatreds that can explode in fascism. It has opposed measures of a progressive foreign policy to make the world safe from war.
>
> The American people need a new people's movement with a policy of basic economic reconstruction for economic security, human welfare and freedom. They need principles and a program to meet the challenge of our modern age to build, out of the achievements of science and technology and of American equalitarian traditions, a new world of greater equality, liberty and justice.
>
> *The Great Challenge*
> The achievements of science and technology can make humanity's dream of the good life for all come true. It is no longer necessary that any human beings should be ill-fed, ill-clothed, ill-housed, overworked; that there should be unemployment and want in the midst of plenty; that people should live in economic dependence and insecurity, ignorance and ugliness.
>
> Our productive forces have so multiplied, and continue to multiply, that they can gratify *if fully used* all basic material human wants. Machines that move with scarcely the touch of a human hand are constantly being made more efficient, while new inventions in the fields of electronics, of synthetics and plastics are steadily increasing over capacity to produce an abundance of the good things of life. The productive forces will be able to turn out a still larger flow of goods and services to meet human needs with the coming economic application of atomic energy and photosynthesis, which will unlock for men's use the mysteries of nuclear and solar energy.

With this tremendous and increasing productive capacity we can easily end poverty. We can do more: we can rebuild cities, towns and villages, whole regions, remold the American environment into area of convenience and beauty in which freer people co-operate for nobler living. Increasing leisure, and the means to enjoy that leisure as one desires, is possible for everyone: a life of independence, moral worth and dignity for all men and women.

Yet still men and women are tormented by unemployment and insecurity, and by the *fear* of unemployment and insecurity. Starvation and misery stalk most of the world's peoples. Americans have jobs, but they ask, "When will the next depression come?" Humanity lives in dread of a more destructive atomic war as apprehension grows that the new effort for world co-operation and peace may fail.

Mankind is caught in a crisis of institutions and ideas because of failure to adjust them to changes wrought by scientific and technical-economic developments. This crisis is the first universal crisis since the breakdown of feudalism and the emergence of capitalism.

Social change speeds up while progressive ideas and action lag. The depression of the 1930's was a collapse of economic institutions that war only temporarily saved. Fascism is a collapse of human moral values, a monstrous reaction against the ideals and practices of liberal democracy. War ends but the danger of war become worse and the crisis of institutions and values remains. It is either-or: Either the achievements of science and technology will be used through new ideas, new political alignments and new institutions, to build a world of greater security, freedom and peace, or they will be used to destroy man's world.

There is the challenge! We must develop the ideas, the people's movement and the will to meet that challenge now. . . .

## Toward A People's Party

A new people's party will arise if and when the American people want it.

It must not be a party to pay off grudges regardless of basic political needs and timing.

It must not be what communists are working to set up—a "third party" which they can use to bedevil a progressive American policy in foreign affairs.

A new party will arise to meet the American people's urgent economic, social, and world needs. It will arise to call into action again the American people's idealism, which is neither dead nor a spent force but confused, distracted, frustrated; yet alive and ready to infuse social change with moral values.

## Why a New Party?

There is need for unity on political action and policy that represents the interests of all useful functional groups for the release of an economic abundance from which every group will gain.

The dangerous alternative is pressure politics, in which each group carries on its own pressures to achieve its own narrow interests regardless of the interests of every other group. This ends in a cat-and-dog fight for a larger group slice of a shrinking economic pie. The cat-and-dog fight produces chaos, invites a crack-down by government and strengthens reaction.

The new party must be a party of all useful functional groups, from workers and farmers to small businessmen, salaried employees and professional people: on the model of the Co-operative Commonwealth Federation (CCF) of Canada. It cannot be a party of the trade unions alone, for that would split labor off from the rest of the community, thus giving monopoly reaction the numbers with which to fight. It was this split that was the major factor in the coming of fascism in Italy and Germany.

Ours is a two-party country? But so was Britain. So was the United States when the Republican party arose as a third party to become the *first* party. The new party arose out of a deep-going crisis created by the slavery issue. Today a far greater crisis prevails, the first universal crisis since the downfall of feudalism and the rise of capitalism, which offers the opportunity for a new party *providing* its principles and action meet the needs of the crisis.

No third party has won success since the Civil War? That is true. It is also true that no old party has been permanently captured by the progressive forces, from Populism to LaFollette's Progressivism to the New Deal.

An old party may be captured and used for reform. It cannot be captured and used as an instrument for deep-going social changes, for basic redistribution of economic and political power. Such far-flung objectives can be achieved only by a party new in principles and in organization.

*Party of the American Dream*

A new people's party will be a party to realize liberal economic democracy as the American Dream in newer and finer fulfillments. For the American liberal tradition never separated economic from political democracy. . . .

A new people's party will carry the struggle and aspirations of the American Dream to new achievements. It will be a party that learns from the people what they desire, their basic wants, yearnings and values. It will be a party of critical inquiry, flexible and experimental, using co-operative intelligence to limit the areas of inevitable conflicts so that the conflicts may be solved by co-operative intelligence to promote peaceful change for human welfare, and so prevent the party from adopting means that become a barrier to what the people want. It will be a grass-roots party, operating from the local community upward, with widespread individual participation.

Men and women of good-will everywhere! You can, if you will, recapture the American Dream in the newer and finer fulfillments of a greater economic, political and social democracy.

**b. Statement of A. Philip Randolph, National Treasurer of the Committee Against Jim Crow in Military Service and Training, and President of the Brotherhood of Sleeping Car Porters, AFL, New York City, before the United Sates Senate Committee on Armed Services**
Extract from: United States Senate, Committee on Armed Services, *Universal Military Training: Hearings before the Committee on Armed Services*, 80th Cong. 2nd sess., 30 March 1948, 687–89.

In this statement before the U.S. Senate's Armed Services Committee, Randolph strongly condemned racial discrimination in the military and stated that he would actively assist black men who wished to avoid the draft if the military did not become integrated.

> Mr. Randolph: For 25 years now the myth has been carefully cultivated that Soviet Russia has ended all discrimination and intolerance, while here at home the American Communists have skillfully posed as champions of minority groups.
> 
> To the rank and file Negro in World War II, Hitler's racism posed a sufficient threat for him to submit to Jim Crow Army abuses. But this factor of minority group persecution in Russia is not present as a popular issue in the power struggle between Stalin and the United States. I can only repeat that this time Negroes will not take a Jim Crow draft lying down. The conscience of the world will be shaken as by nothing else when thousands and thousands of us second-class Americans choose imprisonment in preference to permanent military slavery.
> 
> While I cannot with absolute certainly claim results at this hour, I personally will advise Negroes to refuse to fight as slaves for a democracy they cannot possess and cannot enjoy.
> 
> Let me add that I am speaking only for myself, not even for the Committee Against Jim Crow in Military Service and Training, since I am not sure that all its members would follow my position. But Negro leaders in close touch with GI grievances would feel derelict in their duty if they did not support such a justified civil disobedience movement, especially those of us whose age would protect us from being drafted. Any other course would be a betrayal of those who place their trust in us. I personally pledge myself to openly counsel, aid, and abet youth, both white and Negro, to quarantine any Jim Crow conscription system, whether it bear the label of universal military training or selective service.
> 
> I shall tell youth of all races not to be tricked by any euphonious election-year registration for a draft. This evasion, which the newspapers increasingly discuss as a convenient way out of Congress, would merely presage a synthetic "crisis" immediately after November 2d when all talk of equality and civil

rights would be branded unpatriotic while the induction machinery would move into high gear. On previous occasions I have seen the "national emergency" psychology mow down legitimate Negro demands.

From coast to coast in my travels I shall call upon all Negro veterans to join this civil disobedience movement and to recruit their younger brothers in an organized refusal to register and be drafted.

Many veterans, bitter over Army Jim Crow, have indicated that they will act spontaneously in this fashion, regardless of any organized movement. "Never again," they say with finality.

I shall appeal to the thousands of white youth in schools and colleges who are today vigorously shedding the prejudices of their parents and professors. I shall urge them to demonstrate their solidarity with Negro youth by ignoring the entire registration and induction machinery.

And finally I shall appeal to Negro parents to lend their moral support to their sons, to stand behind them as they march with heads high to Federal prisons as a telling demonstration to the world that Negroes have reached the limit of human endurance, that, in the words of the spiritual, we will be buried in our graves before we will be slaves.

May I, in conclusion, Mr. Chairman, point out that political maneuvers have made this drastic program our last resort. Your party, the party of Lincoln, solemnly pledged in its 1944 platform a full-fledged Congressional investigation of injustices to Negro soldiers. Instead of that long overdue probe, the Senate Armed Services Committee on this very day is finally hearing testimony from two or three Negro veterans for a period of 20 minutes each. The House Armed Services Committee and Chairman Andrews went one step further and arrogantly refused to hear any at all.

Since we cannot obtain an adequate Congressional forum for our grievances, we have no other recourse left to tell our story to the people of the world by organizing direct action. I do not believe that even a wartime censorship wall could be high enough to conceal news of a civil disobedience program.

If we cannot win your support for your own party commitments, if we cannot right a bell in you by appealing to human decency, we shall command your respect and the respect of the world by our united refusal to cooperate with tyrannical injustice.

Since the military, with their southern biases, intend to take over America and institute total encampment of the populace along Jim Crow lines, Negroes will resist with the power of nonviolence, with the weapons of moral principles, with the good-will weapons of the spirit; yes, with the weapons that brought freedom to India.

I feel morally obligated to disturb and keep disturbed the conscience of Jim Crow America. In resisting the insult of Jim Crowism to the soul of black America, we are helping to save the soul of America. And let me add that I am opposed to Russian totalitarian communism and all its works. I consider it a menace to freedom. I stand by democracy as expressing the Judean-Christian ethic. But democracy and Christianity must be boldly and courageously applied for all men regardless of race, color, creed, or country. We shall wage a relentless warfare against Jim Crow without hate or revenge for the moral and spiritual progress and safety of our own country, world peace, and freedom.

Finally let me say that Negroes are just sick and tired of being pushed around and we just do not propose to take it, and we do not care what happens.

Thank you very much.

## c. A. Philip Randolph Debates George Meany

Extract from: A. H. Raskin, "Meany, in a Fiery Debate, Denounces Negro Unionist," *New York Times*, 24 September 1959, 1. Copyright © by the New York Times Co. Reprinted with permission.

The 1959 AFL-CIO convention was a contentious one. Randolph and the labor organization's president, George Meany, had a testy exchange on the convention floor. Although the official proceedings of the 1959 convention did not contain Meany's outbursts, A. H. Raskin reported his words for the *New York Times*. This article is Rankin's summary of the debate.

> George Meany punctuated a fiery debate tonight over Jim Crow Practices in unions by a shouted denunciation of the merged labor federation's only Negro vice president.
>
> The wrangle over racial discrimination brought the federation's third biennial convention to a stormy close. The target of Mr. Meany's attack was A. Philip Randolph, president of the Brotherhood of Sleeping Car Porters.
>
> Mr. Randolph's insistence that the federation should not tolerate long-established segregated locals, even where Negro members wanted to keep them so infuriated Mr. Meany that he accused Mr. Randolph of seeking to throttle the thinking of Negro unionists.
>
> *Explosion Erupts*
> "Who the hell appointed you the guardian of all the Negroes in America?" the president of the American Federation of Labor and Congress of Industrial Organizations demanded.
>
> The explosion was the third in two days over the touchy issue of Negro dissatisfaction with the pace of the federation's effort to wipe out color bars in its unions. Mr. Meany insisted that no organization in the United States had a greater record of accomplishment in this field than the AFL-CIO.
>
> But Herbert Hill, labor secretary of the National Association for the Advancement of Colored People, charged tonight that the work of the federa-

tion's civil rights department had become an "empty ritual with little significance." He called a series of declarations on equal opportunity and anti-discrimination adopted by the convention "more pious platitudes in a long list of pious platitudes.". . .

The conflict over racial bias grew out of two resolutions introduced by Mr. Randolph, who heads a new national Negro labor council. This is seeking to band together the 1,500,000 Negroes now in unions.

One resolution called for the ouster of the Brotherhood of Railroad Trainmen and the Brotherhood of Locomotive Firemen and Engineers if they failed to act in six months to eliminate constitutional bans on Negro members. The other asked for the "liquidation and elimination" of segregated locals in all AFL-CIO unions.

The resolutions committee suggested a substitute for the first proposal under which the two rail unions would be pressed to fulfill the pledges they had given two years ago to eradicate their color bars, but no time limit would be set.

Mr. Randolph asserted that it "was inconsistent" to expel the Teamsters for corruption and to refuse to expel unions that violated the federation's own constitutional prohibition on racial prejudice. He contended that a color line in any union was a symbol of second-class citizenship and a "mockery of trade union morality."

Other Negro delegates were even more outspoken in their demands that a time limit be fixed for expulsion of the two unions. Frank Evans of the Allied Industrial Workers warned that Negro voters would support "right to work" laws next year if they lost confidence in the federation's sincerity.

George Thomas, a regional director of the United Packinghouse Workers, said Negroes were tired of hearing that the way to get rid of Jim Crow practices was to allow the offenders "a little more time."

A strong defense of the federation's record of accomplishment in lessening discriminatory practices came from Mr. Meany. He noted that in the twenty years since he became secretary-treasurer of the old AFL the number of unions with color bars had dropped from twenty to three.

He said the problem of opening unions to all workers without regard to race or color was as much a responsibility of white workers as it was of Negroes. He noted that the heads of the trainmen and the firemen had both assured him of their determination to keep pressing their organizations to eliminate their "white only" clauses. He said all progress in this direction would end if the federation set a deadline. The sole result, Mr. Meany declared, would be to strengthen the hand of those who wanted to keep the color bar.

Fresh pledges of cooperation in eliminating bias came from the heads of two unions—William P. Kennedy of the trainmen and H. E. Gilbert of the firemen. Mr. Kennedy said his union already had more than 1,000 Negro members despite the constitutional limitation on their admission.

### Conflict Sharpens

The second Randolph resolution stirred up a much sharper conflict. The Resolutions Committee recommended that the word "liquidation" be dropped and the resolution confined to the elimination of segregated locals. Even this version drew a protest from a spokesman for the building trades—Harry C. Bates, president of the bricklayers' union and a federation vice president.

He said his union had Negro locals that had been in existence for more than half a century, that they paid the same wage and [had] working conditions as white locals and that they had no desire to have Mr. Randolph tell them they had to go out of business.

Mr. Meany said he was "quite sure" that the proposed resolution was not intended to compel international unions to force out segregated locals where they had no constitutional right to do so and where the members objected to the change.

He said he was familiar with the situation in the Bates unions and he knew there was no organization in the country that had a better record on the maintenance of equal standards for Negro and white members.

### Randolph Objects

Mr. Randolph objected that he interpreted the resolution as establishing a new policy under which measures were to be taken to get rid of all segregated unions. He said it was not "logical" to allow unions to maintain Jim Crow locals "merely because the members want it." To accept such a view, he declared, would be to say that it would be equally permissible to have Communist-dominated unions or unions under gangster influence if the members wanted such unions.

Mr. Meany objected to this view. He said it put Mr. Randolph in the position of putting the desire of Negro members to maintain their unions in a way that had existed for many years in the same class with allowing unions to tolerate communism or corruption.

He asked Mr. Randolph whether it was his idea of the democratic process "that you don't care what the Negro members think."

### Union Chief Retorts

When Mr. Randolph replied, yes, Mr. Meany retorted angrily:

"That's your policy. Well, that's not my policy. I'm for the democratic rights of Negro members to maintain the unions they want."

It was at this point that Mr. Meany interjected his demand to know who had appointed Mr. Randolph as "the guardian of all the Negro members in America."

Mr. Randolph sought vainly to get the microphone to reply but Mr. Meany berated him for talking about "tolerance" and accused him of insisting on doing all the thinking for Negroes regardless of their own desires. Mr. Randolph finally captured the microphone to explain he did not believe any unionist should have the right to maintain a Jim Crow local because such segregation represented a violation of basic trade union principles.

Mr. Meany conceded that no union under Communist domination could remain in the federation even if its members approved of that leadership but he said that he had to part company with Mr. Randolph when he sought to break up Negro locals that had been in existence many years.

## 5. 1963 March on Washington

### a. A. Philip Randolph's Speech at the 1963 March on Washington

Extract from: *Speeches by the Leaders: The March on Washington for Jobs and Freedom* (New York: NAACP, 1963), 3–4. Reprinted with permission from the A. Philip Randolph Institute.

Perhaps for good reason, Americans tend to remember Martin Luther King, Jr.'s, speech at the March on Washington in 1963. Reprinted here, Randolph's speech also helped Americans realize the importance of civil rights reform and its connection to the broader goals of President Johnson's war on poverty.

> Fellow Americans, we are gathering here in the largest demonstration in the history of this nation. Let the nation and the world know the meaning of our numbers. We are not a pressure group. We are not an organization or a group of organizations. We are not a mob. We are the advance guard of a massive moral revolution for jobs and freedom.
>
> This revolution reverberates throughout the land touching every city, every town, every village where black men are segregated, oppressed and exploited. But this civil rights revolution is not confined to the Negro nor is it confined to civil rights, for our white allies know that they cannot be free while we are not and we know that we have no future in a society in which six million black and white people are unemployed and millions more live in poverty. Nor is the goal of our civil rights revolution merely the passage of civil rights legislation.
>
> Yes, we want all public accommodations open to all citizens but those accommodations will mean little to those who cannot afford to use them. Yes, we want a fair employment practices act but what good will it do if profit-geared automation destroys the jobs of millions of workers, black and white. We want integrated public schools but that means we also want federal aid to education—all forms of education. We want a free democratic society dedicated to the political, economic and social advancement of man along moral lines.

Now, we know that real freedom will require many changes in the nation's political and social philosophies and institutions. For one thing we must destroy the notion that Mrs. Murphy's property rights include the right to humiliate me because of the color of my skin. The sanctity of private property takes second place to the sanctity of human personality.

It falls to the Negro to reassert this profit priority of values because our ancestors were transformed from human personalities into private property. It falls to us to demand new forms of social planning, to create full employment and to put automation at the service of human needs, not at the service of profits—for we are the worse victims of unemployment. Negroes are in the forefront of today's movement for social and racial justice because we know we cannot expect the realization of our aspirations through the same old anti-democratic social institutions and philosophies that have all along frustrated our aspirations.

And so we have taken our struggle into the streets as the labor movement took its struggle into the streets, as Jesus Christ led the multitudes through the streets of Judea. The plain and simple truth is that until we went into the streets the Federal government was indifferent to our demands. It was not until the streets and jails of Birmingham were filled that Congress began to think about civil rights legislation. It was not until thousands demonstrated in the South that lunch counters and other public accommodations were integrated. It was not until the Freedom Riders were brutalized in Alabama that the 1946 Supreme Court decision banning discrimination in interstate travel was enforced and it was not until construction sites were picketed in the North that Negro workers were hired.

Those who deplore our militancy, who exhort patience in the name of a false peace are in fact supporting segregation and exploitation. They would have social peace at the expense of social and racial justice. They are more concerned with easing racial tensions than enforcing racial democracy. The months and years ahead will bring new evidence of masses in motion for freedom. The March on Washington is not the climax of our struggle but a new beginning not only for the Negro but for all Americans who thirst for freedom and a better life.

Look for the enemies of Medicare, of higher minimum wages, of social security, of federal aid to education and there you will find the enemy of the Negro—the coalition of Dixiecrats and reactionary Republicans that seek to dominate the Congress. We must develop strength in order that we may be able to back and support the civil rights program of President Kennedy. In the struggle against these forces all of us should be prepared to take to the streets. The spirit and technique that built the labor movement, founded churches and now guide the civil rights revolution must be a massive crusade, must be launched against the unholy coalition of Dixiecrats and the racists that seek to strangle Congress. We here today are only the first wave. When we leave it will be to carry the civil rights revolution home with us into every nook and cranny of the land and we shall return again and again to Washington in ever growing numbers until total freedom is ours. We shall settle for nothing less and may God grant that we may have the courage, the strength and faith in this hour of trial by fire never to falter.

### b. A. Philip Randolph Introduces His Freedom Budget

A. Philip Randolph, A *"Freedom Budget for All Americans: Budgeting Our Resources, 1966–1975, to Achieve "Freedom from Want"* (New York: A. Philip Randolph Institute, 1966), 1–2. Reprinted with permission from the A. Philip Randolph Institute.

Randolph's Freedom Budget was his last great attempt to influence the course of American politics. The visionary proposal sought to advance the federal government's efforts to improve the lives of poor Americans. One wonders what might have happened if it had been implemented.

Why do we call this a "Freedom Budget"?

We call this a "Freedom Budget" because it embodies programs which are essential to the Negro and other minority groups striving for dignity and economic security in our society. But their legitimate aspirations cannot be fulfilled in isolation. The abolition of poverty (almost three-quarters of whose U.S. victims are white) can be accomplished only through action which embraces the totality of the victims of poverty, neglect, and injustice. Nor can the goals be won by segmental or *ad hoc* programs alone; there is need for welding such *programs* into a unified and consistent *program*.

The main beneficiaries will be the poor themselves. But in the progress everyone will benefit, for poverty is not an isolated circumstance affecting only those entrapped by it. It reflects—and affects—the performance of our national economy, our rate of economic growth, our ability to produce and consume, the condition of our cities, the levels of our social services and needs, the very quality of our lives. Materially as well as spiritually, a society afflicted by poverty deprives all of its citizens of security and well-being.

In this war, too, we encounter the pessimists and the tokenists, those who counsel "gradualism" and those who urge piecemeal and haphazard remedies for deep-rooted and persistent evils. Here again, "gradualism" becomes an excuse for not beginning or for beginning on a base too small to support the task, and for not setting goals; and the scattered, fragmented remedies, lacking priorities and coordination, often work at cross purposes.

In the economic and social realm, no less than in the political, justice too long delayed is justice denied. *We propose and insist that poverty in America can and therefore must be abolished within ten years.*

## c. Randolph's Remarks at his Eightieth-Birthday Party

Extract from: A. Philip Randolph, "A Vision of Freedom," Remarks at his 80th Birthday Dinner, May 6, 1969, Waldorf Astoria Hotel, New York City, in *A. Philip Randolph at 80: Tributes and Recollections* (New York: A. Philip Randolph Institute, 1969), 27–29. Reprinted with permission from the A. Philip Randolph Institute.

At his eightieth birthday, Randolph gave his last major public remarks. He acknowledged the importance of his career in the labor and civil rights movements, and he urged his younger colleagues to continue the struggle to improve the lives of African Americans in particular and members of the working class in general. Significantly, he urged them to engage the struggle through nonviolence.

> I need not tell you how happy I am that you all saw fit to come here, and how much I appreciate your attitude towards the work that I have tried to do.
> 
> I want to salute our lovely friend, Mrs. Martin Luther King, a lady of grace and dignity and great dedication to the cause of the black worker, and to the cause of all other workers.
> 
> I'm also happy to see Governor Rockefeller here, a man I have known for a long time. He and I worked together in developing the movement for a Fair Employment Practices Committee. I remember a luncheon we had at the Pierre Hotel at a time when no one thought the FEPC would ever be realized, and I recall that during the discussion Governor Rockefeller said, "No, No. It can be realized if we fight for it."
> 
> And I am also very glad to see my good friend George Meany at this dinner. I know George Meany very well, and I have great admiration and respect for him. He's a man of his word who does not pretend to be for something when he isn't. But if he commits himself to a program, he will work at it and carry it through. We have worked together over a long period of time, and I think that we have made some progress in the field of Civil Rights.
> 
> And of course my good friend Bayard Rustin. He and I have been in this struggle together now for over twenty-five years, and he's still a young man. He has a genius for organization. I have asked him to work on various marches, and the March of 1963—the biggest ever given in this country—was under Bayard's direction.
> 
> So I am very, very happy that you have all been kind enough to join me on this occasion.
> 
> Our gathering here tonight is an honoring, and for that I am deeply grateful and humbled. But in a more profound sense it is a rededication—to a cause to which I have contributed my energies, and to principles to which I have dedicated my life.

The cause has been the liberation of the Negro in America. I have seen fit in this endeavor to try to establish an alliance between the Negro and the American trade union movement. I have been guided by the belief that Negroes are a working people, and that because of their history on American soil—a history of suffering and tragedy, but also of struggle, endurance, dignity and, ultimately, a history of human triumph—that because of this history they have been a dispossessed people who have often had to migrate thousands of miles in search of the means of subsistence. The labor movement has been the home of the working man, and traditionally it has been the only haven for the dispossessed. And, therefore, I have tried to build an alliance between the Negro and the American labor movement.

I have not been alone in my efforts. In 1925, almost half a century ago, I and my colleagues founded the Brotherhood of Sleeping Car Porters. In our struggle to build the union we faced destitution and continual harassment, but we did build it, and our struggle conferred upon us collectively a certain dignity. With this victory, my brothers and I in the union not only improved the conditions under which we lived and worked, but we were enabled to reach beyond ourselves to our brothers and sisters on the plantations and in the ghettos. We were able to reach out and build a movement of the Negro masses struggling to realize, upon this American soil, the freedom and the justice which they had so long been denied.

The Negro masses awakened in 1941. They challenged the President of the United States to integrate the defense industries and all other places of public employment. And they were victorious. The Negro masses were in motion. They were removing the mark of oppression from their brows and the burden of economic misery from their bodies. This struggle has continued down to the present day. Like a mountain stream that grows in size and momentum as it rushes downward, the struggle of the Negro masses for social and economic equality has become irrepressible. From Memphis, Tennessee, to Charleston, South Carolina, they cannot now be satisfied with anything less than total liberation.

Our ceremony of rededication tonight is to the cause of freedom, but it is also to the principles governing the means by which freedom must be achieved. In my life I have tried to abide by the principles of democracy, nonviolence and integration, but there are some today particularly among our black youth, who would question the validity of these principles in our ongoing struggle. I urge them to reconsider their position and to engage with me in a reaffirmation of these fundamental principles. We must reject confrontationism and together reaffirm the necessity for democratic means of political protest. We must reject violence, and together reaffirm the power and the wisdom of nonviolence. And we must reject racial separatism and together, with the conviction that one day our nation can cease to be divided within itself, reaffirm our abiding faith in integration. We cannot reject these principles without also denying ourselves the possibility of freedom.

Salvation for the Negro masses must come from within. Freedom is never granted; it is won. Justice is never given; it is exacted. But in our struggle we must draw for strength upon something that far transcends the boundaries of race. We must draw upon the capacity of human beings to act with humanity towards one another. We must draw upon the human potential for kindness and decency. And we must have faith that this society, divided by race and by class, and subject to profound social pressures, can one day become a nation of equals, and banish white racism and black racism and anti-Semitism to the limbo of oblivion from which they shall never emerge.

# Index

A. Philip Randolph Institute, 106–7
African Americans: Great Depression, 48–54
discrimination, 30, 32, 40–41, 48–67, 71–90, 92–93, 124, 134; great migration, 8–9; military service, 52–53, 78–83, 150–52; segregation, 4–5, 66
African Methodist Episcopal Church, 2–4, 11, 37
Alexander, Will, 142
Alien Registration (Smith) Act (1940), 71
American Federation of Labor (AFL), 19, 40–41, 43–44, 49–50, 84, 86–88, 115
American Federation of Labor–Congress of Industrial Organizations (AFL–CIO), 100–1, 107, 152–55
American Jewish Congress, 104
American Negro Labor Congress (ANLC), 42
American Railway Union, 27, 36
*Amsterdam News*, 60

Anderson, Marion, 102, 104
*Antioch Review*, 75, 146–50
Army War College, 52
Atlanta, Georgia, 34
Attucks, Crispus, 5
Austin, Texas, 104

Baldwin, Florida, 2–3
*Baltimore Afro-American*, 62
Bates, Harry, 154
Belafonte, Harry, 95
Berkman, Alexander, 70
Bethune, Mary McLeod, 79, 142
Biddle, Francis, 56
Bilbo, Theodore G., 74
Birmingham, Alabama, 63–64, 99, 156
Black Panthers, 106
*Black Worker*, 43, 73, 83, 141–42
Boyd, Louise, 51
Bricklayers Union, 154
Briggs, Cyril V., 17
Brotherhood of Engineers, 32
Brotherhood of Labor, 13
Brotherhood of Locomotive Firemen and Engineers, 32, 87, 153

Brotherhood of Railway and Airline Clerks, 109
Brotherhood of Railway Trainmen, 32, 87, 153
Brotherhood of Sleeping Car Porters (BSCP), 25–46, 47, 50, 53, 57–59, 69, 73, 87, 91, 93, 109–11, 116, 129–37, 152, 159
Brotherhood of Sleeping Car Protective Union, 32
*Brown v. Board of Education* (1954), 92–94
Bunche, Ralph J., 48, 59
Burns, Lucy, 58
Bynum, O. W., 42

Camp Robert Smalls, 54
Carey, Archibald James, 37
Carmichael, Stokely, 106
Carry, Edward F., 37–38, 45
Chalmers, Allan Knight, 65
Chavez, Dennis, 84–85
Chicago, Illinois, 20–21, 23, 26, 32, 34–37, 41, 43, 54, 61–64, 73
*Chicago Defender*, 37, 60, 62, 128, 129–34
Civilian Conservation Corps (CCC), 51
City College of New York (CUNY), 12, 42, 80
Clarksville, Tennessee, 35–36
*Cleveland Gazette*, 62
Cleveland, Grover, 27
Cleveland, Ohio, 20
Cohen, Morris R., 12
Committee Against Jim Crow in Military Service and Training, 78–83, 150
Committee on Participation of Negroes in the National Defense Program, 58
Community Party, 48, 59, 80
Communists, 22, 41–42, 48–49, 56, 59, 97, 150, 154, 155

Congress of Industrial Organizations (CIO), 49–50, 87, 145
Congress of Racial Equality (CORE), 97–98, 106–7
Connor, Theophilus Eugene "Bull", 99
Coolidge, Cavlin, 23, 53–54, 61, 77
Cox, Cortland, 104
Coxey, James S., 58
Coxey's Army, 57–58
Craft, Henry K., 144
Crescent City, Florida, 1, 3, 65
*Crisis*, 18, 20, 56
Crosswaith, Frank, 28, 143
Cullen, Countee, 11
Cullen, Frederick, 11

Davis, Benjamin O., Jr., 54
Davis, John P., 48, 49
Debs, Eugene V., 10, 20, 27
Delany, George W., 28
Dellums, C. L., 43, 110
Democratic Party, 64, 66, 71, 73–75, 77–78, 84, 86, 106–9, 126, 147
Detroit, Michigan, 34, 61
Dewey, John, 75
Dewey, Thomas E., 74
Dickerson, Earl, 62–63
Dixon, Youlen, 52
Domingo, W. A., 17
Doram, Thomas, 51–52
Douglas, Paul, 101
Douglass, Frederick, 5
Du Bois, W. E. B., 7–9, 20–22, 42, 59, 62, 94, 112
Dylan, Bob, 104

Early, Stephen, 54
Eastland, James, 94
Eastman, Max, 21
Eisenhower, Dwight D., 94–96
Elaine, Arkansas, 21
Epworth League, 11–13
Espionage Act (1917), 70

Ethridge, Mark, 64
Executive Order 8802, 61–62, 71, 140–41, 144
Executive Order 9346, 64
Executive Order 9664, 75
Executive Order 9808, 77
Executive Order 9980, 82, 86
Executive Order 9981, 82–83
Executive Order 10925, 99

Fair Employment Board, 86
Fair Employment Practice Committee (FEPC), 62–67, 72, 74, 84, 158
Farmer, James, 97, 99
Federal Bureau of Investigation (FBI), 70–71, 98
Fellowship of Reconciliation (FOR), 81, 92–93
Ford, Henry J., 26
Ford, James W., 56
Fortune, T. Thomas, 17
Frazier, E. Franklin, 48
Freedman's Bureau, 1
Freedom Rides, 81, 98, 156

Gandhi, Mohandas K., 57
Garland Fund, 18, 34, 38
Garvey, Marcus, 22–23, 48, 127–28
German American Bund, 71
Gillem, Alvan C., Jr., 78
Gillem Board, 78
Goldman, Emma, 70
Goldwater, Barry, 107
Gompers, Samuel, 10, 19
Goodman, George, 142
Granger, Lester, 47–48, 58, 79, 81, 142
Grant, Ulysses S., 1–2
Great Depression, 42, 44, 48, 50
Great Suffrage March, 57–58

Green, William, 40–41, 44, 62Hannibal, 5
Harding, Warren G., 77

Harris, Abram, 59
Harrison, Hubert, 17, 20
Hastie, William H., 55–56, 142
Headwaiters and Sidewaiters Society of Greater New York, 15
Hearn, Beaman, 3, 8, 10–11
Hedgeman, Anna Arnold, 65
Hershey, Lewis B., 55
Hicks, Granville, 76
Hill, Herbert, 152
Hill, Norman, 97
Hill, T. Arnold, 53–54, 142
Hillman, Sidney, 60, 142–43
Hillquit, Morris, 18–19
Hime, Chester, 59
Hook, Sidney, 76
Hoover, Herbert C., 58
Hoover, J. Edgar, 70–71
Hotel and Restaurant Employees' Alliance, 40
*Hotel Messenger*, 17
Houghton, James, 89–90
Houston, Charles H., 59, 79
Howard, Perry, 28
Humphrey, Hubert H., 104

Independent Political Council, 12, 15
Industrial Workers of the World, 70
International Association of Machinists, 41
International Brotherhood of Boilermakers (IBB), 52, 87
International Brotherhood of Teamsters, 87
International Longshoremen's Association, 87
Interstate Commerce Commission, 39, 132–33
*Irene Morgan v. Commonwealth of Virginia* (1946), 81, 98

Jacksonville, Florida, 3–5, 9–12
Johnston, Eric, 66

Johnson, Campbell, 55
Johnson, J. Rosamond, 9
Johnson, James Weldon, 5, 9, 17–18, 21
Johnson, Lyndon B., 72, 98–99, 105, 107–9, 155

Kennedy, John F., 72, 98–100, 104–5, 156
Kennedy, Robert F., 98
King, Coretta Scott, 95, 98, 110, 158
King, Martin Luther, Jr., 76, 91, 93–95, 97–100, 104, 106, 112, 155
Knights of Labor, 41
Knox, Frank, 53–54, 61, 142–43
Knudsen, William, 142–43
Ku Klux Klan, 8, 22–23, 125, 127–28

Ladies Auxiliary of the International Brotherhood of Sleeping Car Porters, 43
LaGuardia, Fiorello, 43, 46, 61, 143
Lane, Layle, 143
Landon, Alfred, 45
Lassalle, Ferdinand, 10–11
League for Non–Violent Civil Disobedience Against Military Segregation, 79–83
Lemke, William, 45
Lewis, John L., 49, 87
Lewis, John R., 97, 99, 104
Lewisburg Penitentiary, 81
Lincoln, Abraham, 1, 26, 54, 94, 143
Lincoln Memorial, 59, 64, 94, 102, 104
Lincoln, Robert Todd, 27, 32
Little, Malcolm (Malcolm X), 56, 104–5
Little Rock, Arkansas, 93
Logan, Rayford, 58, 142
Los Angeles, California, 52, 61, 63
L'Ouverture, Toussaint, 5
Luce, Henry R., 66

Marcantonio, Vito, 85
McAdoo, William Gibbs, 30, 32

McCarthy, Joseph P., 70–71, 76
MacGowan, Charles, 87
McKay, Claude, 17, 20–21, 28
McNutt, Paul V., 64
Mansfield, Mike, 104
Marshall Plan, 109
Marx, Karl, 10, 12, 15
May, Benjamin E., 28
March on Washington (1963), 91–116, 155–57, 158
March on Washington Movement (MOWM), 57–67, 81, 84, 111, 137–40, 159
Meany, George, 88–90, 101, 110, 152–55
*The Messenger*, 17–18, 19–23, 25, 34, 42
Methodism, 2–4
Miller, Dorie, 55
Milwaukee, Wisconsin, 92
Mississippi Freedom Democratic Party, 108
Mitchel, John Purroy, 18
Montgomery Improvement Association (MIA), 93, 98
Moore, Fred R., 17
Moore, Morris "Dad," 36
Morris, Paul, 52
Morrow, Edward P., 38–40, 129–31
Morse, Wayne, 79
Murray, Philip, 62
Muste, A. J., 81, 92–93
Mydal, Gunnar, 77

National Association of Colored Graduate Nurses, 55
National Association for the Advancement of Colored People (NAACP), 18, 21–22, 47, 49, 53–54, 56, 58, 59, 62, 65, 73, 79, 91, 93, 97, 104, 107, 152
National Council for a Permanent FEPC (NCPFEPC), 65–66, 84–86
National Council of Negro Women, 55

Index ~ 165

National Education Committee for a New Party (NECNP), 75–77, 146–49
National Industrial Recovery Act (1933), 44
National Labor Relations (Wagner) Act (1935), 45
National Labor Relations Board (NLRB), 44
National Negro Congress (NNC), 48–50, 54, 58–59
National Non–Partisan Political Conference, 73
National Press Club, 101
National Urban League, 18, 47–48, 53, 54, 58, 65, 79, 81, 97, 104, 109
Negro American Labor Council (NALC), 89, 92, 107, 153
*The Negro World*, 128
New York City, New York, 8–19, 34, 36, 43, 46, 61, 63–64, 97, 126–27, 158
*New York Times*, 59, 60, 85–86, 87, 152–55
Ninety–Ninth Pursuit Squadron, 54
Nixon, Richard, ix, 76, 96
Norton, Mary T., 84

Oakland, California, 34, 36, 43
Ocean Hill–Brownsville Controversy, 110
Office of Production Management (OPM), 60
Olney, Richard, 27
Omaha, Nebraska, 21
Omnibus Civil Rights Act (1964), 105
Order of Railroad Conductors and Brakemen, 32
Order of Sleeping Car Porters (OSCP), 45
Ottley, Roy, 63
Owen, Chandler, 15, 17–22, 35, 80, 128

Palmer, A. Mitchell, 17, 70
Parish, Richard, 63, 89, 144
Patterson, Robert, 53–54, 61
Patterson, Robert P., 78
Paul, Alice, 58
Pearl Harbor attack, 55
Perkins, Francis, 143
Peter, Paul, and Mary, 104
*Philadelphia Tribune*, 62
*Pittsburgh Courier*, 39, 58–59, 65, 81, 135–37, 142
*PM*, 82, 142
Powell, Adam Clayton, 144
Powell, Tom, 110
Prayer Pilgrimage for Freedom, 94
President's Committee on Civil Rights, 77, 86
President's Committee on Equal Employment Opportunities (PCEEO), 99
President's Committee on Equality of Treatment and Opportunity in the Armed Services (Fahy Committee), 83
Prinz, Joachim, 104
Progressives, 18, 75, 149
Pullman Company, 20, 25–46, 129–37
Pullman Employee Representation Plan (ERP), 32, 34, 37
Pullman, George, 26–27
Pullman, Illinois, 26
Pullman Porters, 25–46
Pullman Porters and Maids Protective Association (PPMPA), 32

Race riots, 21, 106, 109
Railroad Men's Benevolent Association, 36
Railway and Steamship Clerks Union, 41
Railway Labor Act, 38–40, 45, 130–32
Randolph, Asa Philip: childhood, 1–8, 123; and the Brotherhood of Sleeping Car Porters, 25–46, 47, 50, 53, 57–59, 69, 73, 87, 91, 93,

109–11, 116, 129–37, 159; and Du Bois, 7–8, 20–21; education, 3–6, 12; and the Fair Employment Practice Committee, 47–67; and the Federal Bureau of Investigation, 70–71; Freedom Budget for All Americans, 109, 157; and the labor movement, 40–41, 44, 62, 86–90, 101, 110, 152–55; and Marcus Garvey, 22–23, 127–28; March on Washington Movement, 47–67, 137–46; March on Washington, 1963, 91–112, 155–57; and the military, 20, 72–83, 144, 150–52; and the movement for a permanent FEPC, 66–67, 83–86; Pacifism, 19–21, 40, 53, 107; and politics, 72–78; Prayer Pilgrimage for Freedom, 94; radical years in New York City, 8–23; religion, 6–7, 11, 14–15, 33–34, 94; socialism, 12–13, 14, 15–23, 33–34, 36, 39, 48, 57, 70–71, 84, 104, 124–27; Youth March for Integrated Schools, 94–96

Randolph, Elizabeth, 1–7, 12
Randolph, James W., Jr., 2–4, 6–7, 42
Randolph, James W., Sr., 1–8, 12, 23
Randolph, Lucille (Green), 13–15, 20, 38, 43, 83, 100
Raskin, A. H., 87, 152–55
Rauh, Joseph L., Jr., 61
Reconstruction, 1–5
Red Cross, 53
Republican Party, 61, 74–75, 78, 82, 86, 107, 125, 147, 151
Reynolds, Grant, 78–79
Rockefeller, Nelson A., 66, 158
Rockwell, George Lincoln, 104
Robinson, Jackie, 95
Reuther, Walter, 101, 104
Richberg, Donald P., 38
Roosevelt, Eleanor, 53, 60, 74, 143

Roosevelt, Franklin D., 44, 48, 50, 54–57, 59, 60–62, 70–71, 74, 76–78, 99, 100, 126, 137, 140–42, 147
Rosenberg, Anna, 143
Russell, Richard B., 74, 86
Rustin, Bayard, 63, 80–83, 91–112, 158

St. Louis, Missouri, 34, 40
*St. Louis Argus*, 37, 39
Schuyler, George, 56
Sarnoff, David, 62
Schlesinger, Arthur M., Jr., 76, 100
Scottsboro Nine, 49
Sedition Act (1918), 20–21, 70
Selective Service and Training Act (1940), 54
Shuttlesworth, Fred, 97
*Smith v. Allwright* (1944), 73
Society for the Prevention of Calling Sleeping Car Porters George, 28
Socialism, 10–12, 15, 18–19, 124–27
Socialist Party, 19–20, 76, 124–27
Socialists, 18, 48–49, 57, 71, 75–76, 97
Southern Christian Leadership Conference (SCLC), 91, 93, 97, 99, 104, 106
Southern Conference for Human Welfare, 73
Staupers, Mabel K., 55
Stedman, Seymour, 20
Stimson, Henry L., 55, 61, 142, 143
Strange, Henri, 12
Student Non–Violent Coordinating Committee (SNCC), 97, 104, 106

Taft, William H., 126
Texas, 73
Three Hundred Thirty Second Fighter Group, 55
Till, Emmett, 93
Thomas, George, 153
Thomas, Norman, 76

Tobias, Channing H., 142
Totten, Ashley L., 25, 32, 40, 42
Trotter, Monroe, 53
Truman, Harry S., 72, 74–79, 83, 86, 99, 100
Turner, Nat, 5
Tuskegee, Alabama, 54

Union of Soviet Socialist Republics (USSR), 22, 49, 60, 70, 72, 80, 88, 150
United Automobile Workers, 101
United Federation of Teachers (UFT), 110
United Mine Workers, 87
United Packinghouse Workers, 153
United States Army, 54–55, 71, 78
United States Army Air Corps, 53
United States Coast Guard, 54–55
United States Congress, 60, 66, 79, 83, 84–86, 100, 104–5, 111, 125, 147, 150–52, 156
United States Chamber of Commerce, 66
United States Employment Service (USES), 51
United States Marine Corps, 53–55
United States Navy, 53–55
United States Supreme Court, 45, 73, 81, 92, 98, 156
Universal Military Training Bill (1948), 79
Universal Negro Improvement Association (UNIA), 22
USS *Arizona*, 55
USS *Booker T. Washington*, 55
USS *Frederick Douglass*, 55
USS *Robert L. Vann*, 55

Vann, Robert L., 39, 58–59, 135–37
Vietnam War, ix, 107–9
Voting Rights Act (1965), 105

Walker, Madame C. J., 13
Wallace, Henry, 76
War Department, 53, 54
War Manpower Commission (WMC), 64
Ward, Lester Frank, 15
Washington, Booker T., 7–8, 54
Weaver, Robert C., 60, 142
Webster, Milton P., 35, 37, 39, 41–42, 44, 49, 57, 62–63, 73, 80
Welcome, Ernest T., 13
White, Walter, 47, 49, 53–54, 58–59, 61, 79, 142–43
White, William, 15–16
Wilkins, Roy, 81, 91, 94–95, 97, 99, 104, 110
Williams, Aubrey, 142–43
Williams, Camilla, 102
Wilson, Helena, 43
Wilson, Woodrow, 19, 21, 30, 70, 77, 126
Women's Army Corps (WAC), 55
Women's Economic Council (WEC), 43–44
Woodrow, Isaac, 71, 77
World War (1914–1918), 19–21
World War (1939–1945), 47–67, 69, 72, 78

Young, Whitney, 97, 99–100
Youth March for Integrated Schools (1958, 1959), 94–96
Young Men's Christian Association, 53

# About the Author

**Andrew E. Kersten** is associate professor of history and chair of the Social Change and Development Department at the University of Wisconsin, Green Bay. He is the author of *Race, Jobs, and the War: The FEPC in the Midwest, 1941–1946* and *Labor's Home Front: The American Federation of Labor and World War II* as well as numerous articles.